· THE FILMS OF ·
ELVIS PRESLEY

by Susan Doll

Publications International, Ltd.

Susan Doll holds a Ph.D. in Radio, Television, and Film from Northwestern University. In addition to teaching film courses at several Chicago-area colleges, she is the author of *Elvis: A Tribute to His Life* and *Marilyn: Her Life & Legend*. Ms. Doll has also written for several national film publications.

Copyright © 2001 Publications International, Ltd. All rights reserved. This book may not be quoted in whole or in part by any means whatsoever without written permission from:

Louis Weber, CEO
Publications International, Ltd.
7373 North Cicero Avenue
Lincolnwood, Illinois 60712

Permission is never granted for commercial purposes.

Manufactured in China.

8 7 6 5 4 3 2 1

ISBN: 0-56173-278-8

Library of Congress Catalog Card Number: 91-61572

Credits:
Dolores Balcom Collection: 7, 45, 48 (bottom), 50 (top & center), 58 (top), 61, 62 (bottom), 71, 75, 77, 80 (bottom), 81, 82 (top), 89 (bottom); **Cinema Collectors:** Front cover, 9 (bottom), 10 (bottom), 11, 14 (top), 15 (top left & bottom), 16, 18, 19, 20, 22 (top), 24, 27 (top left & bottom), 30 (top), 31 (top right & bottom), 32 (bottom), 33, 41 (bottom), 54, 67 (bottom), 69, 79 (top), 82 (bottom), 83, 84, 86, 87; **Linda Everett Collection:** 26 (top), 36, 37 (bottom), 40 (bottom), 42, 43, 46, 47, 57, 95 (bottom); **Sharon Fox Collection:** 38 (bottom), 39 (bottom), 50 (bottom), 51 (top left), 60 (center & bottom), 63 (bottom), 64 (bottom), 65 (bottom), 79 (bottom), 93; **Alexandria Miller Collection:** 78 (bottom); **Photofest:** 4, 19 (top right), 37 (top right), 41 (top), 72 (bottom), 73, 76 (bottom); **Ger Rijff Collection:** 8, 10 (top), 12, 14 (bottom), 15 (top right), 23, 26 (bottom), 27, 28, 30 (bottom), 34, 37 (top left), 70 (bottom), 78 (top), 88 (bottom), 89 (top), 96; **Joe Tunzi Collection:** 31 (top left), 55 (top left), 85 (bottom), 92.

CONTENTS

ELVIS ON CELLULOID

Elvis Presley acted in 31 feature films, not one lost money.

No actor has been less appreciated than Elvis Presley; no group of films has been more belittled than Elvis's musical comedies. In countless Presley biographies and career overviews and in most rock 'n' roll histories and analyses, Elvis's films have been written off as mindless, unrealistic, formulaic, and trite. Yet, no Presley picture ever lost money, and through the benefit of cable television and video, audiences still enjoy his 31 features and two concert films, as well as the many documentaries and TV shows and miniseries about his life. This contradiction points to the narrowness of the standard view concerning Elvis's Hollywood career while simultaneously calling for a reevaluation of his films by placing them in context.

Much of the rationale for the usual negative view of Presley's films derives from Elvis himself. Elvis became disillusioned with his film career when he was prevented from reaching his goal. From the moment he took his screen test with producer Hal Wallis in April 1956, the young singer had wanted to be a serious actor. Interviews with Elvis from this early period indicate his desire to work hard, learn from the veteran performers who costarred in his films, and become a dramatic actor—just as singers Frank Sinatra and Bing Crosby had done before him.

In his first four films and in a handful of dramas he starred in after his discharge from the Army, Elvis made great strides toward that goal. The perception around Hollywood at the time—as expressed by Hollywood insiders, in trade magazines, and in fanzines—was that Elvis would step in where James Dean had left off. Dean had died September 30, 1955, leaving vacant his niche, both on the screen and off, as resident Hollywood rebel. The controversy Elvis had generated among the Establishment concerning his sensual performing style, plus the phenomenal following he had with teenagers, made him a natural to fill Dean's shoes. Though the film industry had typed him, Elvis was in good company, fitting the same mold as Dean and the young Marlon Brando. Elvis was considered a worthy candidate for roles in major film productions of the time, including *The Rainmaker, The Way to the Gold,* and *The Girl Can't Help It.*

After the success of the musical comedy *Blue Hawaii* in 1961, Elvis's management team—personal manager Colonel Tom Parker, agent Abe Lastfogel from the William Morris Agency, and film producer Hal Wallis—convinced Elvis that his fans preferred him in lightweight musical vehicles. *Blue Hawaii* contained the formula that most of Elvis's films were based on. In a nutshell, the typical Presley picture was a romantic musical comedy set in an exotic locale. Elvis's musical talents were exploited by featuring a song every 12 to 13 minutes.

Elvis quickly became disappointed with what he termed the "Presley travelogues," complaining about their unrealistic storylines and their repetitive nature.

He also found the tendency for his character to burst into song at any time to be particularly offensive. Friends, relatives, and acquaintances have all testified to his bitterness at having been thrust into so many musical comedies.

TEEN FLICKS

Many Presley biographers have used Elvis's negative opinion of his Hollywood career to suggest that none of his films from the 1960s, except perhaps *Flaming Star, Blue Hawaii,* and *Viva Las Vegas,* have any intrinsic value. The logic seems to be that if Elvis was ultimately disappointed in the bulk of his movies, then they should be dismissed as worthless fluff. This shortsighted viewpoint of Elvis's prolific film career has resulted in little effort to put his movies in perspective or to understand why all of them turned a profit. Elvis may have grown bitter about his film career for a variety of reasons, but his fans responded favorably to his movies, as they still do today. Placing the films in a context outside of Elvis's personal feelings helps show them in a different light.

In Presley lore and literature, Elvis's later films are most often referred to as "vehicles," stressing the negative connotations associated with that word. But appearing in a series of vehicles does not necessarily constitute a bad career move. A vehicle is a film built around a star's image, and it usually provides a concrete character type to associate with the star. In addition, a vehicle furnishes a showcase for a performer to do his or her specialty; in this regard, musical stars tend to benefit more than other actors from appearing in vehicles. Throughout the history of Hollywood, a number of well-respected musical and comedy stars, including Astaire and Rogers and Abbott and Costello, have appeared in movies tailor-made to their specific singing, dancing, or comic abilities. In this context, producer Hal Wallis's conception of a series of musical comedies to display the talents of Elvis Presley is not unusual.

Elvis was not the only rock 'n' roll star to appear in a series of lightweight musical vehicles during the 1960s. Several rock 'n' roll and pop performers—from Frankie Avalon to Herman's Hermits—starred in a variety of musicals aimed at youthful audiences. Some of these musicals featured pop-flavored songs that sounded more like some Hollywood executive's idea of what rock music should be. Other musicals included the songs of well-known rock 'n' roll bands of the era.

Most prominent among these was the series of beach movies produced by American International Pictures and starring Frankie Avalon and Annette Funicello. The first—*Beach Party,* released in 1963—was so successful, it launched four others: *Muscle Beach Party, Bikini Beach, Beach Blanket Bingo,* and *How to Stuff a Wild Bikini.* In each film, Funicello played DeeDee, who spent most of the plot trying to keep Frankie, played by Avalon, in check. Each film was set at Malibu Beach, California. The characters whiled away the days on the beach and danced away the nights at a local hangout.

Though the low-budget origins were often apparent, these films seemed to capture the pleasures of youthful pastimes and the spirit of the surfing music so popular in the early 1960s. Several denizens of the "surfin' sound," including the Hondells and the Kingsmen, made guest appearances in this series of vehicles. In addition, well-known film actors from older generations, such as Buster Keaton and Mickey Rooney, represented an adult point of view.

When the beach began to look a bit too familiar, the party moved to the ski slopes. A whole new sub-series was born after producer Gene Corman at American International decided to use a ski resort for the setting of *Ski Party*. Other musicals made use of a college setting, including *Get Yourself a College Girl* and *C'mon, Let's Live a Little.*

Some of the British rock groups of the era were also packaged into movie vehicles to showcase their specific style of music. Peter Noone's band, Herman's Hermits, made a splash with their feature musical *Hold On.* Two feature films from The Beatles, *Help!* and *A Hard Day's Night,* belong to this genre as well, though Richard Lester's direction lifts them above the exploitative nature of these types of films.

In the mid-1960s, a number of serious feature films, which had obviously been inspired or influenced by the success of these youth-related musical vehicles, began to crop up. Melodramas with bigger budgets and scripted around youthful topics exploited the popularity of these idols of American youth. Nancy Sinatra and Peter Fonda appeared in *The Wild Angels,* a drama about the destructive actions of a motorcycle gang. Perhaps the best remembered is *Where the Boys Are,* a romantic melodrama with Dolores Hart and George Hamilton.

Elvis's vehicles differ slightly from most of these youth-oriented musical comedies and dramas because they were designed for a family audience. Thus, Elvis's films include children and characters from older generations. There is also less emphasis on such youthful elements as fashion and slang. Despite this, Elvis's movies fit quite well into this youth-related genre. Many of Elvis's costars were featured in the beach and ski party movies. Some of the producers and directors responsible for the beach and ski party movies also worked on Elvis's films.

In terms of specific settings and plots, many of Elvis's films emulated what was happening in other youth-related musicals. When spring break in Ft. Lauderdale and other resort areas became a popular subject, as in *Where the Boys Are* and *Palm Springs Weekend,* Elvis starred in his own Ft. Lauderdale adventure called *Girl Happy.* When the mod scene in England and Europe was all the rage, Elvis appeared in *Double Trouble,* which featured the swinging discotheques of London and Amsterdam (as re-created on Hollywood sound stages) as a backdrop. Even the considerable number of beach-related films that Elvis made, including *Blue Hawaii* and *Clambake,* was the result of the popularity of beach movies.

Seen within the context of this youth-oriented genre, Elvis's films make perfect sense. They even stand out because of the high-quality production values. In a review of *Easy Come, Easy Go,* a critic for *Variety* praised Elvis's movies for this reason: "Anyone who has seen similar films recognizes the superior quality of Presley's films: the story makes sense; the songs are better, and better motivated; cast and direction are stronger; production values are first-rate."

COSTARS AND BIT PARTS

Elvis's films make fascinating viewing for other reasons too. Movie buffs have found the supporting casts of his movies to feature a number of interesting costars. Though often saddled with perky ingenues as costars, Elvis sometimes played opposite a strong leading lady who had no problem holding her own on-screen with the hot, young idol. Among this group were Barbara Stanwyck, Carolyn Jones, and others.

Often young actors and actresses who may have already established themselves in Hollywood but would later go on to more prominent careers were featured in secondary roles in Elvis's movies. Walter Matthau, for example, was making only his sixth screen appearance when he played opposite Elvis in *King Creole* as the mobster determined to ruin everyone's life. Costarring in *Kid Galahad* was Charles Bronson, who would later become an international star as well as one of the highest paid actors in the world. Some of these young performers later found fame as stars of popular television programs. Barbara Eden, for example, before popping out of a bottle in *I Dream of Jeannie,* costarred in *Flaming Star* early in her career.

A veritable who's who of acting talent—totally unknown at the time but now considered big names in films and television—appeared in Elvis's films in bit parts. Looking for these popular performers in various films adds to the overall viewing experience. To name just two: Teri Garr can be spotted briefly in a bit part as a showgirl in *Viva Las Vegas*; Raquel Welch made her film debut in *Roustabout* as a college girl.

OFFSCREEN ROMANCES

Early in his Hollywood career, Elvis secured a reputation for dating one or more of his costars during the production of each film. Rumors about the crushes he harbored for various actresses abound. Much was obviously manufactured, but some was true.

Of all his relationships with his costars, Elvis's romance with Ann-Margret was perhaps the most serious. During the production of *Viva Las Vegas,* Elvis and the red-haired starlet set the publicity mill grinding when they began showing up together at restaurants and clubs around Las Vegas. Another costar who caught Elvis's eye was singer-dancer Juliet Prowse, who played Elvis's love interest in *G.I. Blues.* Elvis made her his love interest offscreen as well. Other actresses whom Elvis dated during his career in Hollywood included Joan Blackman and Yvonne Craig, among others.

Some actresses were notable for not dating Elvis during film production. Donna Douglas, costar of *Frankie and Johnnie,* was a religious and spiritual person who impressed Elvis because she was so well read. Elvis tried desperately to get costar Shelley Fabares to go out with him during the production of *Girl Happy,* but she was involved with record producer Lou Adler, whom she later married.

A FINAL WORD

If Elvis was so disillusioned with Hollywood, why did he continue to star in these movies? Unfortunately, there is no satisfactory answer to this big question. Most of Elvis's commercial endeavors from this period, including films and albums, were financially successful no matter how hastily manufactured. This profitability served to validate the path Elvis and the Colonel chose for Elvis's career. Also, the Colonel tended to tie Elvis up with three-film contracts with a number of studios. So even when Elvis wanted to stop making films, he was contractually obligated to star in several more. Rather than bemoaning Elvis's squandered talent and reflecting on the missed opportunities of his film career, it is more fruitful to accept what Elvis offered.

Smooching and surf, an unbeatable combination for Elvis in Live a Little, Love a Little.

CAST

Vance Reno . . . .Richard Egan
Cathy Reno . . . .Debra Paget
Clint Reno . . . . .Elvis Presley
Mr. Siringo . .Robert Middleton
Brett Reno . .William Campbell
Mike Gavin. . . .Neville Brand
Martha Reno . . . .
. . . . . . .Mildred Dunnock
Major Kincaid . .Bruce Bennett
Ray Reno . . . . .James Drury
Ed Galt. . . . . .Russ Conway
Mr. Kelso . . . . .Ken Clark
Mr. Davis . . . . .Barry Coe
Pardee Fleming . . .L.Q. Jones
Jethro . . . . . .Paul Burns
Train Conductor . Jerry Sheldon

CREDITS

Twentieth Century-Fox

Produced by David Weisbart

Directed by Robert Webb

Screenplay by Robert Buckner

Based on a story by
Maurice Geraghty

Photographed in CinemaScope
by Leo Tover

Music by Lionel Newman;
vocal supervision by Ken Darby

Songs written by Vera Matson
with Elvis Presley

Released November 15, 1956

While waiting to do a scene from his first feature film, Love Me Tender, *Elvis enjoys a rare private moment.*

THE FILMS OF ELVIS PRESLEY

LOVE ME TENDER

STORYLINE

In this western drama set immediately after the Civil War, Elvis appears in the secondary role of Clint Reno. This was the only time in his acting career that Elvis received second billing. Clint, the youngest of the four Reno brothers, stayed behind to run the family farm during the war while his older brothers were off fighting for the Confederacy. Star Richard Egan plays Vance Reno, the eldest brother whom the family believes to have been killed in battle. Upon returning home, Vance is shocked to discover that Clint has married Vance's former sweetheart, Cathy, played by Debra Paget. The love triangle, complicated by the greedy actions of some unscrupulous ex-Confederates, eventually pits brother against brother, resulting in Clint's death. The downbeat ending is tempered by the brothers' reconciliation as Clint dies in Cathy's arms.

BEHIND THE SCENES

Elvis's first experience as a Hollywood actor was closely followed in the entertainment press from the day he was assigned a role in *Love Me Tender* until the day the film was released. The close scrutiny affected the outcome of the film in several ways. Originally called *The Reno Brothers*, this western drama was retitled after a number of articles announced that advanced sales for "Love Me Tender"—one of the songs recorded for the film—exceeded a million copies. It was the first time advanced sales for a single release had ever surpassed the million mark, and the producers capitalized on the publicity by changing the film's title.

The enormous amount of press coverage also affected the film's conclusion. During production, fanzines leaked that Elvis's character was supposed to die near the end of the film. As originally shot, the final scene features Mother Reno solemnly ringing the dinner bell as her three remaining sons toil in the fields. Pain and loss are registered on the faces of Mother Reno and Cathy, who mourn the death of Clint. Elvis's legion of fans were disturbed by the news that their idol was to be killed off in

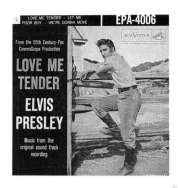

The song "Love Me Tender" was based on the 1861 folk ballad "Aura Lee."

SONGS

We're Gonna Move

Love Me Tender

Let Me

Poor Boy

Elvis tried to romance costar Debra Paget, but she rejected his advances.

Elvis signs an autograph for one of the film's extras.

Richard Egan, Debra Paget, and Elvis appear in the famous death scene, which raised the ire of Elvis's fans.

his first film. In an attempt to counter an "adverse public reaction," Twentieth Century-Fox shot an alternative ending in which Clint is spared. For reasons known only to the producers, this second ending was rejected. A compromise ending was used instead. Clint is killed as called for in the original script, but the final shot superimposed a ghostly close-up of Elvis as Clint crooning "Love Me Tender" as his family slowly walks away from his grave. The fans were then left with a final image of Elvis doing what he was famous for—singing.

Prior to the film's premiere at the Paramount Theater in New York, a 40-foot likeness of Elvis as Clint Reno was erected atop the theater's marquee. Part of the ceremony surrounding the unveiling of the huge cutout included placing the world's largest charm bracelet, which measured nine feet, around the figure's wrist. The charms depicted various events in Elvis's career, and the bracelet was a giant replica of one being merchandised across the country. Some fans attending the unveiling carried placards that complained about Elvis's on-screen death, but Presley biographers have speculated that Colonel Tom Parker, the singer's notorious manager, passed them out to garner even more publicity.

If the promotion surrounding *Love Me Tender* generated excitement among Elvis fans, it generated loathing among the critics. Reviewers around the country were lying in wait for the film, and many were brutal in their assessment of Elvis's performance. In a particularly scathing review for *Time* magazine, one critic compared Elvis's acting and screen presence to that of a sausage, a "Walt Disney goldfish," a corpse, and a cricket—all in the same brief review. Many did not confine their criticism to Elvis's screen performance. Critics used the opportunity to reiterate the same complaints the Establishment had always hurled at Elvis, including his singing style, his hair, his Southern background, and his fanatical following.

If Elvis cried over the mean-spirited reviews, then he cried all the way to the bank. The film recouped its production costs within three days of release, guaranteeing that Elvis's Hollywood future would be lucrative.

RICHARD EGAN
*A rugged leading man for
Twentieth Century-Fox, Egan
held an M.A. in theater from
Stanford and had taught public
speaking before arriving in
Hollywood in 1949. His
experience as a teacher and actor
proved beneficial to Elvis, as
Egan took the young singer under
his wing and served as an
unofficial tutor. Egan's greatest
success in Hollywood occurred
during the 1950s when he starred
in many action-oriented films.
During the 1960s, he turned to
television acting. Egan died
in 1987.*

*Left, top: Elvis as Clint and
Debra Paget as Cathy
are featured in one of
the film's few
lighthearted scenes.
Left, bottom: Though
Love Me Tender is set
in the post-Civil War era,
Elvis's musical numbers
are closer to rock 'n' roll.*

THE FILMS OF ELVIS PRESLEY

Deke Rivers . . . .Elvis Presley
Glenda Markle . .Lizabeth Scott
Walter (Tex) Warner . . . . . .
. . . . . . .Wendell Corey
Susan Jessup. . . .Dolores Hart
Carl Meade . . .James Gleason
Jim Tallman . . .Ralph Dumke
Teddy . . . . . . .Skip Young
Skeeter . . . . . .Paul Smith
Wayne . . . . . . .Ken Becker
Daisy Bricker . . . .Jana Lund
Harry Taylor . . . .Vernon Rich
Mr. Castle . . .David Cameron
Mrs. Gunderson . .Grace Hayle
Mr. Jessup . . .William Forrest
Mrs. Jessup . . . .Irene Tedrow
Sally . . . . . . .Yvonne Lime
Eddie (Bass Player) . .Bill Black
Musician (Drummer) . . . . .
. . . . .D.J. Fontana
Musician (Guitar Player) . . . .
. . . . .Scotty Moore
Bit . . . . . . .Barbara Hearn

CREDITS

Paramount Pictures
Produced by Hal B. Wallis
Directed by Hal Kanter
Screenplay by Herbert Baker
and Hal Kanter
Based on a story
by Mary Agnes Thompson
Photographed in VistaVision
and Technicolor
by Charles Lang, Jr.
Music by Walter Scharf
Vocal accompaniment by
The Jordanaires
Choreography by
Charles O'Curran
Released July 30, 1957

Contrary to popular belief, Elvis received his first screen kiss in Loving You,
not Love Me Tender. *Here, Jana Lund performs the honors.*

THE FILMS OF ELVIS PRESLEY

LOVING YOU

Elvis felt more comfortable in the role of Deke Rivers than he had as Clint Reno since the role was based on his real-life career experiences. The musical drama opens as Deke—a truck driver with a natural talent for really belting out a song—teams up with press agent Glenda Markle, played by Lizabeth Scott, in hopes of becoming the next singing sensation. Deke begins his new singing career as the opening act for a down-and-out country-and-western band headed by Glenda's ex-husband. It soon becomes apparent that the female faction of the audience just can't get enough of Deke either on stage or off. Glenda capitalizes on Deke's sensual appeal by providing him with customized costumes and arranging publicity stunts. Deke is torn between the attraction he feels toward Glenda and the genuine affection he has for the band's lead singer, Susan, played by Dolores Hart in her film debut. When Deke discovers that Glenda has been manipulating him personally and professionally, he becomes confused and runs away. A wiser and more mature Deke returns just in time to perform at a major televised concert, which serves as his introduction to the big time.

BEHIND THE SCENES

Elvis's acting had definitely improved by the time he completed the role of Deke Rivers. Partly, he was more experienced this time out, but also the role had been tailor-made for the young singer. The film showcased Elvis's best musical talents, and the plot was loosely based on his own life —a practice producer Hal Wallis would continue in the future. At the time, this practice proved invaluable to Elvis's career. Since Elvis was so maligned in the press as a figure of controversy and rebellion, the people in charge of his career took on the task of remolding his image. By telling parts of Elvis's life story through the familiar form of the Hollywood rise-to-success film, older audiences saw that the singer was not all that different from entertainers of the past.

An original lobby card from Loving You.

SONGS

Got a Lot o' Livin' to Do

(Let's Have a) Party

(Let Me Be Your) Teddy Bear

Hot Dog

Lonesome Cowboy

Mean Woman Blues

Loving You

Dancing on a Dare
(sung by Hart's character)

Detour
(sung by Hart's character)

The Yellow Rose
(sung by Hart's character)

Candy Kisses
(performed by the
Rough Ridin' Ramblers)

To ensure that the film captured the essence of Elvis's life as a performer, Wallis sent director/co-scriptwriter Hal Kanter to observe Elvis's live appearance on the radio program *Louisiana Hayride* on December 16, 1956. Kanter followed Elvis around for a few days in Memphis and then in Shreveport, Louisiana, where the *Hayride* program was based. Kanter was able to capture the chaos, exhilaration, and confusion that surrounds an up-and-coming popular singer.

In addition to capturing the highs of an entertainer's life, Kanter also worked a number of lows into the storyline, suggesting a "price of fame" theme. While Deke is dining in a restaurant, for example, fans interrupt his meal to ask him to perform, and they then become resentful when he refuses—a reference to Elvis's own real-life lack of privacy. In another scene, fans write love notes in lipstick on Deke's car, which recalls the many times fans had ruined the finish on Elvis's vehicles by leaving similar testimonies in lipstick and nail polish.

To further equate Elvis with Deke, Kanter and Wallis allowed some of Elvis's family and friends to appear in the film in cameos and bit roles. His parents, Vernon and Gladys, appear as members of the audience in the final production number. Real-life band members Scotty Moore, Bill Black, and D.J. Fontana have bits as Deke's band members.

The most obvious similarity between the real-life Elvis and the fictional Deke was the controversy both generated because of their performing style. The film explains that the controversy surrounding Deke is based on a misunderstanding involving miscalculated publicity stunts. This was central to the production team's attempt to make Elvis more acceptable to mainstream audiences. Showing Deke as misunderstood implies that Elvis was also misunderstood. Structuring Deke's success along the same formula as other films about entertainers implies that Elvis's real-life success is just a variation on the same theme. Just as Glenda tells the community leaders in *Loving You* that Deke's music is as fun and innocent as the Charleston was in the 1920s, so the producers of *Loving You* were telling 1950s America to relax—the Deke Rivers/Elvis Presley story was really just a modern-day version of the Al Jolson story.

Elvis performs "Teddy Bear," one of the film's highlights.

Elvis's parents, Gladys and Vernon Presley, had small cameos in the film's final musical number.

HAL B. WALLIS
Wallis, a respected veteran of the film industry, began as a publicity man for Warner Bros., working his way up to executive producer in charge of production by 1933. In 1944, he became an independent producer. As an independent, Wallis had a reputation for fostering new talent. Among those whose screen careers he helped were Kirk Douglas, Shirley MacLaine, and Elvis Presley. Wallis died in 1986.

Left, top: *Two of Elvis's real-life backup musicians had bit roles. Scotty Moore is seated on the far right; D.J. Fontana is seated next to him in the striped coat.* Left, bottom: *Elvis, as Deke Rivers, rocks an audience while Lizabeth Scott, as Glenda Markle, watches the crowd's reaction.*

THE FILMS OF ELVIS PRESLEY

CREDITS

Metro-Goldwyn-Mayer
Produced by Pandro S. Berman
Directed by Richard Thorpe
Screenplay by Guy Trosper
Based on a story by Ned Young
Photographed in CinemaScope
by Robert Bronner
Music by Jeff Alexander
Most songs by Mike Stoller
and Jerry Leiber
Released October 17, 1957

Jailhouse Rock's most famous production number was choreographed by Elvis himself.

JAILHOUSE ROCK

STORYLINE

Jailhouse Rock successfully capitalized on the rebellious side of Elvis's persona, which was an aspect of his image still making headlines at the time of the film's release. As the embittered Vince Everett, Elvis portrayed the most volatile, as well as the most exciting, character of his film career. After accidentally killing a man in a barroom brawl, Vince serves a manslaughter sentence in the state penitentiary, making him cynical and self-centered. While Vince is in prison, former country singer Hunk Houghton, played by character actor Mickey Shaughnessy, takes the young man under his wing and teaches him how to play the guitar. After his release, Vince stumbles onto a hot, new singing style. With the help of record promoter Peggy Van Alden, played by Judy Tyler, he takes the entertainment industry by storm. Later, Hunk joins Vince's entourage, which becomes larger as the ambitious young singer claws his way to the top. Unfortunately, Vince leaves Peggy behind, despite her love for him. Attempting to teach the arrogant lad a lesson, Hunk punches Vince in the throat, injuring his vocal cords. A repentant Vince then realizes his love for Peggy, and his voice is miraculously restored.

BEHIND THE SCENES

If *Loving You* attempted to present Elvis as a sensitive, misunderstood young man, then *Jailhouse Rock* was meant to showcase Elvis Presley the rebel. Elvis's character—Vince Everett—is self-centered, overly aggressive toward women, and somewhat greedy. Though Vince exhibits a change of heart during the movie, it is his unruly behavior and defiant attitude that many remember from the film. Nowhere is his brash behavior more evident than in the scene where he recklessly grabs Peggy to kiss her. "How dare you think such cheap tactics work with me," she chides, pushing him away. "Them ain't tactics, honey, that's just the beast in me," he drawls in a provocative delivery guaranteed to make every girl in the theater swoon.

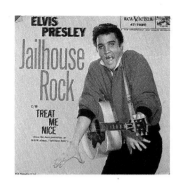

The single "Jailhouse Rock" was number one on the pop charts for seven weeks.

SONGS

Young and Beautiful

I Want to Be Free

Don't Leave Me Now

Treat Me Nice

Jailhouse Rock

(You're So Square) Baby, I Don't Care

One More Day (sung by Shaughnessy's character)

Yet, Vince Everett was ultimately just a character that Elvis portrayed on-screen. Elvis's behind-the-scenes behavior during the production of *Jailhouse Rock* belied the rebellious attitude of his on-screen persona.

More than once Elvis gallantly came to the rescue of his costars when they were caught in potentially dangerous circumstances. During the scene in which Peggy Van Alden, played by Judy Tyler, was supposed to run out the door of a small nightclub after an angry Vince, the young actress accidentally ran into the plate glass door, thrusting her arm through it. Elvis quickly turned back, caught Judy, and blocked the door before it swung back and hit her again. In another instance, Elvis and a property man were passing by Jennifer Holden's dressing room when they heard her scream. An electric heater had shorted out, and her room caught on fire. Elvis and the prop man dashed into the dressing room and quickly doused the flames. Elvis carried the panicky starlet to safety.

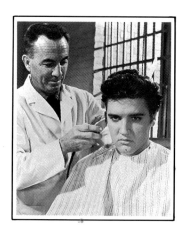

Fans wept and parents cheered at this well-known scene. The question remains: Was it Elvis's real hair or just a wig?

Far from being greedy or selfish, Elvis was known throughout his life for his generosity toward friends, acquaintances, and even complete strangers. After the principle photography on *Jailhouse Rock* had been completed, Elvis decided to present each member of the crew with a small token of his gratitude. Each of the 250 crew hands received large envelopes inscribed with, "Thanks to the entire cast and crew." Inside each envelope was a personally autographed photo of Elvis, plus a small gift.

Elvis's sensitivity was exposed to the entire country shortly after the production had wrapped. Elvis was devastated when costar Judy Tyler and Gregory Lafayette, her husband of only a few months, were killed in a gruesome car crash near Billy the Kid, Wyoming. When told of the accident, Elvis broke down and cried. His reaction was disclosed to a reporter who wrote about it for the *Memphis Commercial Appeal*. Other papers around the country then picked up the incident. The article revealed a pensive young man, who murmured in an unguarded moment, "I remember the last night I saw them. They were leaving on a trip . . . . All of us boys really loved that girl. She meant a lot to all of us. I don't believe I can stand to see the movie we made together now. . . ."

Elvis and costar Jennifer Holden get acquainted between scenes.

DEAN JONES
Though primarily known as a leading man in family comedies for the Disney studios, Jones has actually experienced a diverse career. He began as a blues-type singer before drifting into acting during the mid-1950s; thus, his role as a rock 'n' roll disc jockey in Jailhouse Rock *was not farfetched. Already familiar with the music, Jones was assisted in his deejay delivery by real-life jocks Ira Cooke and Dewey Phillips. Jones starred in a variety of films, from horror features to bedroom farces, before beginning his association with Disney in the mid-1960s.*

Left, top: Elvis wept upon hearing the news of costar Judy Tyler's untimely death.
Left, bottom: Could the hound dogs featured in this shot of Elvis and Mickey Shaughnessy be a sly reference to Elvis's most famous song?

CAST

Danny Fisher . . . .Elvis Presley
Ronnie . . . . . .Carolyn Jones
Nellie . . . . .Dolores Hart
Mr. Fisher . . . . .Dean Jagger
"Forty" Nina . . . .
. . . . .Liliane Montevecchi
Maxie Fields . . .Walter Matthau
Mimi Fisher . . . .Jan Shepard
Charlie LeGrand . . .Paul Stewart
Shark . . . . . . .Vic Morrow
Sal. . . . . . . .Brian Hutton
Dummy . . . . . .Jack Grinnage
Eddie Burton . . .Dick Winslow
Mr. Evans . . .Raymond Bailey
Mr. Primont . . .Gavin Gordon
Ralph . . . . .Val Avery
Dr. Patrick . . . .
. . . . .Alexander Lockwood
Dr. Michael Cabot . . . . . .
. . . . . . .Sam Buffington
Hotel Clerk . . . . .Ned Glass
Doorman . . . .Candy Candido
Street Vendor . . . .Kitty White

CREDITS

Paramount Pictures

Produced by Hal B. Wallis

Directed by Michael Curtiz

Screenplay by Herbert Baker and
Michael Vincente Gazzo

Based on the novel
A Stone for Danny Fisher
by Harold Robbins

Photographed by Russell Harlan

Music by Walter Scharf

Vocal accompaniment by
The Jordanaires

Choreography by
Charles O'Curran

Released July 2, 1958

Elvis snuggles with Carolyn Jones, who later starred in the hit television series The Addams Family.

KING CREOLE

STORYLINE

Elvis received the best reviews of his career with his portrayal of Danny Fisher in this musical drama set in New Orleans. Danny is dissatisfied with the financial situation of his poverty-stricken family and blames his father for their problems. He sweeps up at a nightclub to earn extra money—a job that places the impressionable young man in the company of some shady characters. An encounter with Ronnie, a local gangster's moll portrayed by Carolyn Jones, results in Danny's expulsion from high school. On the job that night at the club, Danny runs into Ronnie and gangster Maxie Fields, played by Walter Matthau, who insist that Danny sing a song. Danny's natural talent attracts the attention of the owner of the King Creole night spot, who offers him a job. Danny is at a crossroads. He is torn between the love of good girl Nellie, played by Dolores Hart, and his attraction to the ill-fated Ronnie. Danny is also torn between his desire for a singing career and the temptation to join a street gang. A violent altercation with the gang's leader, played by Vic Morrow, leaves Danny with a serious knife wound. After Ronnie nurses him back to health, a jealous Maxie shoots her in cold blood. Maxie in turn is shot by a gang member Danny had once befriended. Danny returns to singing at the King Creole, reconciled with his family and with Nellie.

BEHIND THE SCENES

Generally considered Elvis's best narrative film, *King Creole* benefited from the talents of several Hollywood notables. Producer Hal Wallis chose one of his closest associates, the well-respected Michael Curtiz, to direct the film. Best known as the director of *Casablanca*, Curtiz was an expert craftsman known for his deft handling of a wide variety of film genres during his 30-year career. The tight control over the many twists and subplots of *King Creole* reflects Curtiz's expertise. Other Hollywood veterans who made up the crew included cinematographer Russell

Elvis's films were also big hits in Europe, as this French fanzine indicates.

SONGS

Crawfish

Steadfast, Loyal and True

Lover Doll

Trouble

Dixieland Rock

Young Dreams

New Orleans

Hard Headed Woman

King Creole

Don't Ask Me Why

As Long as I Have You

Turtles, Berries and Gumbo
(sung by street vendors)

Banana
(sung by Montevecchi's character)

Harlan, who photographed the film in a dark, moody lighting style that captured the seedy but seductive atmosphere of the French Quarter. The level of experience that Wallis, Curtiz, and Harlan brought to the production of *King Creole* would never be matched in another Presley feature.

Elvis's supporting cast represented some of the finest Hollywood actors of the 1950s. Carolyn Jones, who appeared as Ronnie, had received an Oscar nomination the previous year for her brief but electrifying performance in *The Bachelor Party*. Such notable character actors as Paul Stewart (the butler in *Citizen Kane*), Dean Jagger (the retired general in *White Christmas*), and Vic Morrow (the juvenile delinquent in *The Blackboard Jungle*) helped maintain a high caliber of acting; thus, any rough edges in Elvis's performance would go unnoticed. Though relatively unknown in 1958, Walter Matthau would go on to star in such classic comedies as *The Odd Couple* and *The Sunshine Boys*.

While on location in New Orleans, the crowds of curious onlookers and excited fans were so large that Wallis had to arrange for tighter security. The entire top floor of the Roosevelt Hotel was booked for the film's cast. Pinkerton guards patrolled the floor, the elevators, and the staircase to keep overzealous fans from Elvis. As an added precaution, Wallis insisted that the elevator should not be allowed to run to the top floor to prevent any outsiders from getting onto Elvis's floor. Simply returning to his hotel room at the end of the day proved difficult for Elvis because there were always large crowds waiting for him in the lobby. To avoid the crowds, Elvis entered an adjacent building, climbed out a window, crossed the roof, and entered his hotel via the fire escape.

In his autobiography, Wallis recalled a particularly sad moment for Elvis. Eager to try some of New Orleans' famous cuisine, Elvis was disappointed to learn he could not dine at the legendary Antoine's because no one could guarantee crowd control. During his stay in New Orleans, Elvis ordered room service. This isolation was part of the price Elvis paid for stardom, and by this point, it had begun to affect his lifestyle.

Director Michael Curtiz and producer Hal Wallis discuss a scene. Curtiz is best known as the director of Casablanca.

This scene is taken from an original lobby card for King Creole.

DOLORES HART

Hal Wallis discovered Dolores Hart when she was just 18 years old. Wallis recognized what her niche in films could be when he saw her blush during an interview in his office. "You don't find many girls who blush," he noted. He thus cast Hart in innocent ingenue roles, as in her two Elvis films, Loving You *and* King Creole. *Later, she tended to be cast as an honest, levelheaded character who is pure in heart. Hart shocked Hollywood in 1963 when she entered the Benedictine order to become a nun.*

Left, top: Elvis poses with his female costars (from left): Jan Shepard, Dolores Hart, Carolyn Jones, and Liliane Montevecchi. Left, bottom: Elvis rehearses with The Jordanaires, who provided backup vocals for many of his films.

Elvis in costume for the film. Several other titles, including Cafe Europa, *were considered and discarded before settling on* G.I. Blues.

G.I. BLUES

In his first musical comedy, Elvis stars as lady-killer Tulsa MacLean, an Army sergeant stationed in West Germany. Tulsa and his buddies hope to make enough money to open a small nightclub upon their return to civilian life. At the urging of his pals, Tulsa accepts a bet with a group of G.I.s to win the heart of Lili, a beautiful cabaret dancer at the Cafe Europa. Lili, played by dancer Juliet Prowse, has a reputation for resisting soldiers, so Tulsa's finesse with females is required to break through her cool exterior. Just as Tulsa realizes that he is in love with Lili, she finds out that she has been the target of a wager. Lili manages to overcome her anger to help Tulsa out during a troublesome night of babysitting for a friend's infant son. At a rehearsal for an Armed Forces show, Lili discovers that Tulsa has called off the bet, proving he truly loves her.

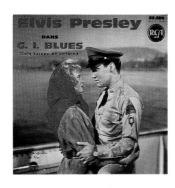

This single, taken from the film's soundtrack, was released in Europe.

BEHIND THE SCENES

G.I. Blues marks the debut of the new Elvis Presley. Taking advantage of the good publicity Elvis received for serving his tour of duty in the Army, the Colonel launched a new, more clean-cut image for Elvis after his discharge. Film critics and movie magazines alike noticed the differences in Elvis's image, including changes in his personal appearance and attire. Gone were the sideburns the press had found so offensive, and gone was the flashy, hip attire. The new look was more conservative—befitting Hollywood's latest leading man.

As produced by Hal Wallis, *G.I. Blues* borrowed some details from Elvis's personal life to flesh out his character, Tulsa MacLean. This was nothing new for Wallis and his production team. They had used a similar strategy in Elvis's pre-Army features, particularly *Loving You* but also in *King Creole*. The intent was to attract Elvis's legion of fans who were already familiar with Elvis's life. In *G.I. Blues*, Tulsa MacLean is an entertainer soon to be released from the Army. Tulsa is stationed in West Germany and is a member of a tank division, just as Elvis had been.

SONGS
What's She Really Like
G.I. Blues
Doin' the Best I Can
Frankfort Special
Shoppin' Around
Tonight Is So Right for Love
Wooden Heart
Pocketful of Rainbows
Big Boots
Didja Ever

The King of Rock 'n' Roll meets two Scandinavian princesses on the set of G.I. Blues.

Despite borrowing tidbits from Elvis's own life, the film differed a great deal from the singer's previous efforts. The major change was in terms of genre: His pre-Army films had been musical dramas; *G.I. Blues* was a musical comedy. His pre-Army films were based on previously published novels or stories; *G.I. Blues* was specifically written for the screen and followed a simpler, more formulaic story structure. Elvis's management team and the film's production team also attempted to soften the singer's screen image. His character is older and more mature, and in one sequence he sings "Wooden Heart" to a group of children at a puppet show; in another he baby-sits an infant. Other notable differences included toning down Elvis's controversial performing style in hopes of capturing a family audience, not just teenage fans. In *G.I. Blues*, Elvis no longer swung his hips when he sang, long-legged costar Juliet Prowse did it for him. Even though some of the songs in *G.I. Blues* are fast-paced, they lack the hard-driving sound, emotional delivery, and sexual connotations of his pre-Army recordings. "Mean Woman Blues" had given way to "Pocketful of Rainbows."

A great deal of publicity was generated during the production of *G.I. Blues*, much of designed to showcase the new Elvis. Visiting dignitaries from other countries were paraded through the set at a rapid rate. Elvis met the King and Queen of Nepal as well as Princess Margrethe of Denmark, Princess Astrid of Norway, and Princess Margaretha of Sweden. Elvis met so many foreign notables during the film's production that he had difficulty getting the protocol straight. He once asked, "Is this another of those highness deals?"

Juliet Prowse and Elvis chat with a visitor between scenes.

The changes in terms of image and film genre do not mean that *G.I. Blues* was an inferior film, which many Presley biographers have implied. It remains a well-crafted musical comedy with a number of solid songs and a strong female costar. The only negative result of the film was that Elvis would be discouraged from making other types of movies. *G.I. Blues* is considered the prototype for the other Presley musicals, which, unfortunately, declined in quality as the decade progressed.

NORMAN TAUROG

Norman Taurog was responsible for nine Elvis Presley features— more than any other director. Elvis always favored Taurog, probably because of his kind nature and lack of ego. After a particularly difficult scene, Taurog would pass out candy bars to the cast and crew. Like Hal Wallis, Taurog was a Hollywood veteran. He directed many major stars in more than 70 films during six decades, winning an Oscar in 1931 for Skippy. Taurog, who died in 1981, said of Elvis, "I was always proud of his work, even if I wasn't proud of the scripts. I always felt that he never reached his peak."

*Left, top: Elvis sings "Didja Ever" in the film's finale.
Left, bottom: Elvis and costar Robert Ivers know their way around a tank.*

CAST

Pacer Burton . . . .Elvis Presley
Roslyn Pierce . . . . .Barbara Eden
Clint Burton . . . .Steve Forrest
Neddy Burton. .Dolores Del Rio
Sam Burton. . . .John McIntire
Buffalo Horn . .Rudolph Acosta
Dred Pierce. . . .Karl Swenson
Doc Phillips . . . .Ford Rainey
Angus Pierce . .Richard Jaeckel
Dorothy Howard . .Anne Benton
Tom Howard. . . . .L.Q. Jones
Will Howard . . .Douglas Dick
Jute . . . . . . .Tom Reese
Ph'Sha Knay . .Marian Goldina
Ben Ford. . . .Monte Burkhart
Mr. Hornsby . . . .Ted Jacques
Indian Brave . . .Rodd Redwing
Two Moons. . . . .Perry Lopez
Matt Holcom . . . .Roy Jenson
Indian Brave . . . . .Red West

CREDITS

Twentieth Century-Fox

Produced by David Weisbart

Directed by Don Siegel

Screenplay by Clair Huffaker
and Nunnally Johnson

Based on the novel
Flaming Lance
by Clair Huffaker

Photographed in DeLuxe Color
and CinemaScope by
Charles G. Clarke

Music by Cyril J. Mockridge

Vocal accompaniment by
The Jordanaires

Released December 20, 1960

*To play Pacer Burton, Elvis donned dark makeup and brown contact lenses.
The lenses were quickly discarded when his eyes looked too dark on film.*

FLAMING STAR

S T O R Y L I N E

As Pacer Burton, Elvis starred in one of the few dramatic roles of his career. A western with an excellent supporting cast of some of Hollywood's most notable actors, *Flaming Star* tells a story of racial intolerance toward Native Americans in the Old West. Pacer, the son of a white father and Kiowa mother, lived a peaceful existence with his racially mixed family until members of the Kiowa nation massacre the Burtons' neighbors. Pacer's loyalties are divided between the white man's civilized world and the freer existence of the Kiowas. When white settlers murder his mother, played by longtime Hollywood star Dolores Del Rio, Pacer joins the Kiowas. But the confused young man finds no peace with the tribe, particularly after they kill his father and seriously wound his brother. Pacer abandons the Kiowas to rescue his brother; he sends the injured brother back to town and then prepares to battle the pursuing Indians. The next morning, a wounded Pacer returns to his brother to bid farewell because he has seen the flaming star of death and knows he must ride into the mountains to die.

B E H I N D   T H E   S C E N E S

Some Presley biographies have indicated that the role of Pacer Burton was originally written for Marlon Brando, adding credence to the commonly held notion that Elvis could have been another Brando if he had not been stuck with so many musical comedies. This is too simplistic an interpretation of what really transpired in terms of the script for this film. Hollywood projects often go through many studios, changing focus and casts at every turn, and this was certainly the case with *Flaming Star*.

In 1958, Twentieth Century-Fox had purchased the rights to Clair Huffaker's newest novel, which was not yet complete. Titled *The Brothers of Broken Lance* at the time, the storyline focused on two characters instead of one. Marlon Brando and Frank Sinatra were offered and

This album featured the two songs from the soundtrack plus other odds and ends. The album, released in 1968, was not distributed in conjunction with the film.

S O N G S

Flaming Star

A Cane and
a High Starched Collar

Elvis visits his mother's people, the Kiowas.

Elvis and director Don Siegel take a coffee break.

Angry over his treatment by other ranchers in the valley, Elvis, as Pacer Burton, takes a hard line.

accepted the two main roles, that of the Burton brothers. Later, negotiations broke down with both stars, and neither decided to star in the film. When the novel was completed, it was retitled *Flaming Lance*. While the novel was being adapted to the script, the focus of the film shifted to one brother. Elvis was the only actor offered the role of Pacer Burton. During production, the film went through a number of title changes, including *Flaming Heart*, *Black Star*, and *Black Heart*, before finally being released as *Flaming Star*. The role Elvis accepted differed from the original conception of the character that had been offered to Brando. To imply that Elvis replaced Brando in this film is misleading.

In *Flaming Star*, Elvis was given the opportunity to prove himself as a serious actor. That this film was considered an important feature is indicated by the choice of director, scriptwriter, and supporting cast. Don Siegel, who had directed the science-fiction classic *Invasion of the Body Snatchers* and who would later direct *Dirty Harry*, guided Elvis through *Flaming Star*. With author Clair Huffaker, respected scriptwriter Nunnally Johnson adapted the screenplay. The cast included the legendary Dolores Del Rio, a screen star in Mexico as well as in America. *Flaming Star* was her first appearance in an American film in 18 years.

Though the movie provided Elvis with one of his few opportunities to act, the film's producers and Colonel Parker were nervous about the reaction of fans. To hedge their bets, they attempted to insert four songs into the film. Director Siegel was not pleased with that decision and fought to keep the songs out even after he had shot them. The final version of the film contains two songs. Siegel realized from his experiences with *Flaming Star* that Elvis's chance of pursuing a serious acting career was doomed. He later told *Rolling Stone* magazine, "I found {Elvis} sensitive and very good, with the exception that he was very unsure of himself. . . . He felt he could have done better things. And his advisors —namely the Colonel—were very much against doing this kind of straight role. They tried to get him to sing throughout the picture. Obviously, they didn't want him to get off the winning horse. But when I was able to calm him down, I thought he gave a beautiful performance."

BARBARA EDEN

Though Barbara Eden did not end up with Elvis's character at the end of Flaming Star, *she played the only ingenue role in the film. Eden made her screen debut in 1956 in a drama titled* Back from Eternity, *but* Flaming Star *was her first major film. After costarring in a number of popular but insignificant films, including* Five Weeks in a Balloon, Ride the Wild Surf, *and* Voyage to the Bottom of the Sea, *Eden achieved stardom on the small screen in the TV series* I Dream of Jeannie.

Left, top: Flaming Star *represented an attempt by Elvis to become a serious actor.*
Left, bottom: *Elvis performs one of only two musical numbers left in the final cut of* Flaming Star.

WILD IN THE COUNTRY

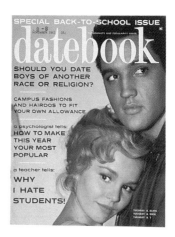

Fanzines played up the fact that Elvis and Tuesday Weld had been romantically linked prior to the film's release.

SONGS

Wild in the Country
I Slipped, I Stumbled, I Fell
In My Way
Husky Dusky Day

Hope Lange as "older woman" Irene Sperry, who causes a scandal when she falls for Elvis.

STORYLINE

The part of Glenn Tyler in *Wild in the Country* represented Elvis's last serious role in a film by a significant director. The story opens as Glenn, a Southern boy from a rural, poverty-stricken background, has just been released from juvenile hall. Central to the character of Glenn is that the brooding young man is at a crossroads in his life, and he must choose the path most suitable for him. His choices are represented by three women. The sensuous Noreen, played by Tuesday Weld, is Glenn's country cousin who urges Glenn to stay with his own kind. She offers passion and good times, but such a carefree existence allows little thought for the future. Hope Lange costars as Irene Sperry, the court-appointed psychiatrist assigned to Glenn's case, who recognizes in him the raw talent of a budding writer. She encourages him to attend college but causes a scandal when she falls in love with her charge. Finally, childhood sweetheart Betty Lee, played by Millie Perkins, selflessly places Glenn's future above her own needs, urging him to leave town and attend college. She is prepared to lose him that he may have an education and a secure future. Glenn follows Betty Lee's advice, asking her to wait for him.

BEHIND THE SCENES

Tuesday Weld was one of the trio of female costars (Hope Lange and Millie Perkins were the other two) who provide strong supporting performances. Only 17 years old during the film's production, Weld was the hottest starlet in Hollywood. As wild as she was beautiful, Weld had already had romances with two of her costars in the film—Elvis and 45-year-old John Ireland. So much was written about Weld during the early 1960s that fact and fiction fuse into one long publicity parade. Many of the rumors were spread by Weld herself, who enjoyed thumbing her nose at Hollywood's entertainment columnists. She abandoned the Hollywood scene shortly after *Wild in the Country* to study at the Actors Studio in New York.

CAST

Glenn Tyler . . . .Elvis Presley
Irene Sperry . . . .Hope Lange
Noreen. . . . . .Tuesday Weld
Betty Lee Parsons . . . . . .
. . . . .Millie Perkins
Davis . . . . .Rafer Johnson
Phil Macy . . . .John Ireland
Cliff Macy . . .Gary Lockwood
Rolfe Braxton. . .William Mims
Dr. Underwood . . . .
. . . . .Raymond Greenleaf
Monica George . . . .
. . . . .Christina Crawford
Flossie . . . .Robin Raymond
Mrs. Parsons. . . .Doreen Lang
Mr. Parsons . . . .Charles Arnt
Sarah the Maid. .Ruby Goodwin
Willie Dace . . . . .Will Cory
Professor Joe B. Larson. . . . .
. . . . .Alan Napier
Judge Parker . . . .
. . . . . .Jason Robards, Sr.
Sam Tyler . . . .Harry Shannon
Hank Tyler . . . . . .Red West
Mr. Longstreet . . .Pat Buttram

CREDITS

Twentieth Century-Fox
Produced by Jerry Wald
Directed by Philip Dunne
Screenplay by Clifford Odets
Based on a novel by
J.R. Salamanca
Photographed in DeLuxe Color
and CinemaScope by
William C. Mellor
Music by Kenyon Hopkins
Released June 22, 1961

Top: *Tuesday Weld played Noreen, who tries to persuade Elvis to forget college.*
Bottom: *Millie Perkins costarred as Betty Lee, Elvis's childhood sweetheart in* Wild in the Country.

CAST

Chad Gates . . . .Elvis Presley
Maile Duval . . .Joan Blackman
Sarah Lee Gates . . . .
. . . . . .Angela Lansbury
Abigail Prentice. .Nancy Walters
Fred Gates . . .Roland Winters
Jack Kelman . . . .John Archer
Mr. Chapman . . . .
. . . . . .Howard McNear
Tucker Garvey . . .Steve Brodie
Enid Garvey. . . . .Iris Adrian
Waihila . . . . .Hilo Hattie
Ellie Corbett. . .Jennie Maxwell
Selena Emerson . .Pamela Kirk
Patsy Simon . . . .
. . . . . .Darlene Tompkins
Beverly Martin . .Christian Kay
Carl Tanami. . . . .Lani Kai
Ernie Gordon. . . .Jose Devega
Ito O'Hara . . . .Frank Atienza
Wes Moto . . . .
. . . . .Ralph (Tiki) Hanalei
Party Guest. . . . .Red West

CREDITS

Paramount Pictures

Produced by Hal B. Wallis

Directed by Norman Taurog

Screenplay by Hal Kanter

Photographed in Technicolor
and Panavision by
Charles Lang, Jr.

Music by Joseph J. Lilley

Vocal accompaniment by
The Jordanaires

Choreography by
Charles O'Curran

Released November 22, 1961

Elvis and Joan Blackman marry in a Hawaiian wedding ceremony in the beautiful final sequence of Blue Hawaii.

BLUE HAWAII

STORYLINE

Blue Hawaii, a musical comedy originally titled *Beach Boy*, became the most successful film of Elvis Presley's career. Elvis stars as Chad Gates, whose wealthy family owns a successful pineapple plantation in Hawaii. At the beginning of the film, Chad has just returned from the Army, and his family is eager for him to pursue the family business. Instead, Chad lands a job as a guide in the tourist agency where girlfriend Maile, played by Joan Blackman, also works. His new vocation not only allows him to use his knowledge of the Islands' most beautiful sites but also affords him enough time to cavort on the beach with his native Hawaiian buddies. Tension mounts as Chad's blue-blooded mother, played by Angela Lansbury, objects to his job, his girlfriend, and his beach-loving friends. Chad eventually proves a success in the tourist business, and he finally wins the approval of his family by marrying Maile and making plans to open his own tourist agency.

BEHIND THE SCENES

Much of *Blue Hawaii* was filmed on location in America's 50th state, which had only joined the union in 1959. The new state of Hawaii was as eager for the exposure in a major Hollywood film as the producers and actors were to shoot there. Such beautiful Hawaiian locations as Waikiki Beach, Ala Moana Park, Lydgate Park, and the Coco Palms Resort Hotel were used in the film; also used were such unglamorous locations as the Honolulu jail.

Despite working primarily on location, the producers experienced only minor problems. The first occurred just prior to shooting. Juliet Prowse, who had been Elvis's costar in the successful *G.I. Blues*, was cast opposite Elvis in the role of Maile Duval. She was loaned to Paramount from Twentieth Century-Fox for the film. Eleven days before filming was to begin in Hawaii, Prowse declared that she was not going to report to work until three demands were met. Prowse wanted her Fox makeup

A fanzine helps promote Elvis's most popular film.

SONGS

Blue Hawaii

Almost Always True

Aloha Oe

No More

Can't Help Falling in Love

Rock-a-Hula Baby

Moonlight Swim

Ku-u-i-Po

Ito Eats

Slicin' Sand

Hawaiian Sunset

Beach Boy Blues

Island of Love (Kauai)

Hawaiian Wedding Song

Nancy Walters (center) costarred as a school teacher who wanted to teach Elvis a few things.

In his musical comedies, Elvis often broke into song at anytime, a characteristic that he hated about his films. Here, he sings "Island of Love (Kauai)" to a tour group.

man to do her makeup, she wanted the traveling expenses of her secretary to be paid by the producers, and she wanted a change made in her contract regarding her billing. Wallis replaced Prowse with the lesser known Joan Blackman.

Shooting on location was always a problem when Elvis was the star of a film because increased security was necessary to protect him from fans. When Elvis arrived in Honolulu, thousands of fans nearly broke down the barricades before the singer was whisked to his hotel. Since mobs waited around his hotel daily, security guards were on duty around the clock. Again, Elvis was disappointed that he could not visit the sites, and he often looked out his window to watch others strolling along the beach. One morning he saw a heartfelt message written in the sand by the very fans he needed to be protected from. Elvis was touched by the simple message: "We love you, Elvis!"

One minor incident that caused an unnecessary delay was actually the fault of Colonel Parker. Rain moved in on the location one day, causing the crew to wait hours for a break in the weather. The rain finally stopped, and just as director Taurog was able to roll camera on Elvis running out of the surf, Parker rushed in front of the camera yelling, "Cut, cut!" Proper etiquette on the set maintains that only the director can stop the action. Hal Wallis and Taurog were furious and demanded to know what could be important enough for Parker to halt the shot. The Colonel slyly pointed out that Elvis was wearing his own watch during the scene. The contract spelled out that Elvis was to provide no part of his wardrobe, including jewelry. If Taurog wanted to keep any part of the shot that had just been done, Wallis and Paramount would have to pay Elvis an extra $25,000. Taurog asked Elvis to remove his watch, and the shot was redone. Why the Colonel pulled this power play is not known.

The success of *Blue Hawaii* sealed Elvis's fate in terms of his film career. Though *Flaming Star* and *Wild in the Country* had not lost money, neither had they set the box office afire. The Colonel used the box-office grosses of *Blue Hawaii* to convince Elvis that his fans preferred him in musical comedies.

ANGELA LANSBURY

Lansbury was only 35 years old when she played Elvis's mother in Blue Hawaii. *More a character actress than a movie star, Lansbury played Laurence Harvey's mother in* The Manchurian Candidate *though she was only three years older than Harvey. Lansbury has been recognized as a major acting talent throughout most of her career, garnering the first of three Oscar nominations for her screen debut in* Gaslight *in 1944. Later, Lansbury would receive Tony Awards for her performances in the Broadway musicals* Mame *and* Sweeney Todd.

Left, top: *At a luau, Elvis as Chad Gates, croons a tune to Joan Blackman as Maile.*
Left, bottom: *Juliet Prowse was originally slated for Joan Blackman's role in* Blue Hawaii.

FOLLOW THAT DREAM

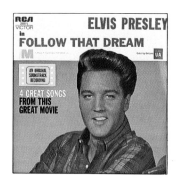

This extended-play record features four of the songs in the film.

SONGS

What a Wonderful Life
I'm Not the Marrying Kind
Sound Advice
On Top of Old Smokey
Follow That Dream
Angel

Joanna Moore played a social worker interested in Elvis's character.

STORYLINE

In a deviation from his usual musical comedy character, Elvis was Toby Kwimper, a L'il Abner-type in a family of bumbling rural Southerners. The Kwimpers, consisting of Pop, Toby, and several adopted orphans, claim squatter's rights along an unopened stretch of highway and open a small business renting fishing equipment. Gamblers attempt to take advantage of the Kwimpers' trusting nature. Eventually, Toby routs the hoods. In the meantime, beautiful social worker Alicia Claypoole, played by Joanna Moore, investigates the Kwimpers' situation to determine if the children are receiving proper care. Alicia's attention to Toby angers Holly Jones, played by Anne Helm, who has been in love with the handsome young man since childhood. After Toby declines the social worker's amorous advances, Alicia attempts to take the children away from Pop Kwimper. Toby and Pop plead their case in a comic courtroom scene, and the judge decides in their favor.

BEHIND THE SCENES

Follow That Dream was filmed in sunny Florida, marking one of the few times a Presley feature was shot entirely on location. The head of the Florida Development Commission was pleased to have the film shot in his state, declaring, "This movie will sell Florida around the world."

Shooting on actual Florida beaches added a touch of authenticity to the movie, but location filming did give the producers minor headaches. The temperature soared passed 100 degrees one week, making it difficult on the cast, crew, and equipment. Elvis had to change his shirt 22 times in one day because he was perspiring so heavily. Another problem involved difficulties obtaining gambling equipment for a couple of scenes, because all gambling was illegal in Florida in 1961. One day, a local politician and a couple of anonymous gamblers just showed up on the set with the necessary equipment. No questions were asked.

CAST

Toby Kwimper . . . .Elvis Presley
Pop Kwimper. . . . .
. . . . . .Arthur O'Connell
Holly Jones . . . . .Anne Helm
Alicia Claypoole . .Joanna Moore
Carmine . . . . .Jack Kruschen
Nick . . . . .Simon Oakland
Judge Wardman . . . .
. . . . . . .Roland Winters
H. Arthur King. . .Alan Hewitt
George Binkley . . . .
. . . . .Howard McNear
Jack. . . . . . .Frank de Kova
Mr. Endicott. . .Herbert Rudley
Eddy Bascombe. . .Gavin Koon
Teddy Bascombe . .Robert Koon
Al. . . . . . .Robert Carricart
Blackie . . . . . .John Duke
Governor . . .Harry Holcombe
Bank Guard . . . . .Red West

CREDITS

United Artists
Produced by David Weisbart
Directed by Gordon Douglas
Screenplay by Charles Lederer
Based on the novel
Pioneer, Go Home
by Richard Powell
Photographed in DeLuxe Color
and Panavision by
Leo Tover
Music by Hans J. Salter
Released May 23, 1962

Top: *This scene from a lobby card shows the Kwimper family in* Follow That Dream. Bottom: *In the final courtroom sequence, the humble Kwimpers win out over hypocritical bureaucrats.*

THE FILMS OF ELVIS PRESLEY

KID GALAHAD

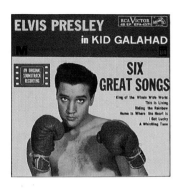

All six songs from the film were featured on this extended-play soundtrack.

To prepare for his role, Elvis trained with former junior welterweight champion Mushy Callahan.

S T O R Y L I N E

A remake of the 1937 drama of the same title starring Edward G. Robinson and Humphrey Bogart, *Kid Galahad* features Elvis as boxer Walter Gulick. Though not a great boxer, Walter has a powerful right hook and can take a lot of punches. Gig Young costars as Willy Grogan, a down-and-out gambler who owns the training camp where Walter spars with other boxers. Willy decides to groom Walter to be a professional boxer, hoping to make enough money to pay off his gambling debts to gangster Otto Danzig, chillingly portrayed by character actor David Lewis. Willy's relationship with Walter changes when Walter falls in love with Willy's sister, Rose, played by Joan Blackman, Elvis's costar from *Blue Hawaii*. Willy does not want Rose to be involved with Walter, so he allows Walter to be overmatched for his next fight by a superior boxer. Just before the big fight, Willy realizes that he has compromised his moral integrity. He and Walter rid themselves of Danzig and his shady dealings, while Walter goes on to win the match.

B E H I N D   T H E   S C E N E S

For his role as boxer Walter Gulick, Elvis eagerly began training before the start of production. He prepared for his boxing scenes as a real fighter might prepare for a fight. He did road work, went on a strict protein diet, punched bags, sparred for hours with professionals, and lost 12 pounds in the process. Coaching the young singer was Mushy Callahan, the junior welterweight champion from 1926 to 1930. Callahan had been plying his skills around Hollywood for some time, having coached actors Kirk Douglas, Errol Flynn, and others in boxing-related films. Callahan was always conscious of training an actor so that his boxing skills suited the character. Callahan praised Elvis for his natural athletic skills—at least in the publicity for the film. "He's got a good physique and excellent coordination," the old pro revealed in an interview. "He never boxed before but he picked it up quick because of his karate training."

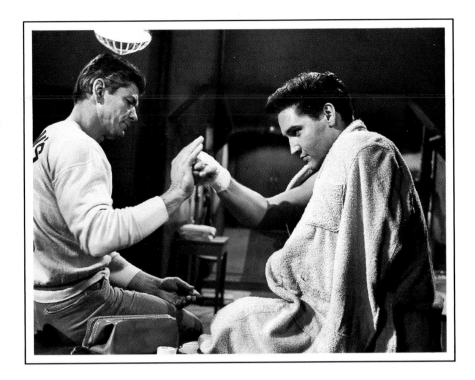

CAST

Walter Gulick . . . .Elvis Presley
Willy Grogan . . . .Gig Young
Dolly Fletcher . . .Lola Albright
Rose Grogan . . .Joan Blackman
Lew Nyack . . .Charles Bronson
Mr. Lieberman . . . .Ned Glass
Mr. Maynard . .Robert Emhardt
Otto Danzig . . . .David Lewis
Joie Shakes. . . .Michael Dante
Mr. Zimmerman . .Judson Pratt
Mr. Sperling . .George Mitchell
Marvin . . . . .Richard Devon
Ralphie . . . . .Jeffrey Morris
Father Higgins . .Liam Redmond
Jerry the Promoter. .Roy Roberts
Peter J. Prohosko. .Ralph Moody
Ramon "Sugarboy" Romero . . .
. . . . .Orlando de la Fuente
Romero's Manager. . . . . . .
. . . . .Frank Gerstle
Frank Gerson . . . . .Ed Asner
Fight Announcer . . . .
. . . . .Jimmy Lennon
Bit . . . . . . .Sonny West

CREDITS

United Artists
Produced by David Weisbart
Directed by Phil Karlson
Screenplay by William Fay
Based on a story by
Francis Wallace
Photographed in DeLuxe Color
by Burnett Guffey
Music by Jeff Alexander
Released August 29, 1962

Top: *Charles Bronson helps Elvis train for a fight in this musical remake of a 1937 drama.*
Bottom: *In* Kid Galahad, *Joan Blackman played opposite Elvis for a second time.*

THE FILMS OF ELVIS PRESLEY

GIRLS! GIRLS! GIRLS!

Stella Stevens tries her luck at charming Elvis, but to no avail.

SONGS

Girls! Girls! Girls!

I Don't Wanna Be Tied

We'll Be Together

A Boy Like Me, A Girl Like You

Earth Boy

Return to Sender

Because of Love

Thanks to the Rolling Sea

Song of the Shrimp

The Walls Have Ears

We're Coming in Loaded

Dainty Little Moonbeams

Girls! Girls! Girls (reprise)

Never Let Me Go
(sung by Stevens's character)

The Nearness of You
(sung by Stevens's character)

Baby, Baby, Baby
(sung by Stevens's character)

Mama
(sung by Elvis, Goodwin, Puglia, and Valenty)

STORYLINE

Ross Carpenter, Elvis's character in *Girls! Girls! Girls!* epitomizes the type of role Elvis is most associated with—the handsome, carefree bachelor with a colorful occupation. Ross works as a charter boat pilot who moonlights as a nightclub singer to buy a sailboat that once belonged to his father. Wealthy Laurel Dodge, played by Laurel Goodwin, falls hard for Ross and secretly buys the sailboat for him. When Ross discovers that Laurel has purchased the boat, his pride is damaged, and he sails off by himself. Laurel quickly follows in a boat piloted by wealthy Wesley Johnson, portrayed by Jeremy Slate, who turns out to be a wolf in tailored clothing. Ross rescues Laurel from Wesley's clutches, realizing that he loves her. Ross asks Laurel to sell the sailboat so that he can feel free to marry her and build a new boat.

BEHIND THE SCENES

Girls! Girls! Girls! reteamed Elvis with producer Hal Wallis and director Norman Taurog. The combination of Wallis, Taurog, and Presley had been responsible for two of Elvis's biggest grossing films, *G.I. Blues* and *Blue Hawaii.* Paramount used this detail in the promotional material sent to theater owners across the country. Included in this promotional package were some "hot tips" on how to bolster attendance for the film. For theaters playing the film during football season, it was suggested that a cheering squad from local high schools be used to draw attention to the film. The squad should perform the cheer, "Rah! Rah! Rah! Girls! Girls! Girls!" either in front of the theater or on the football field. Another suggestion was known as the "Girl Triplets Bally" and involved hiring a set of triplets to parade in front of the theater. The triplets were to be dressed alike and carry identical signs reading, *"Girls! Girls! Girls!* Starring Elvis Presley." This suggestion concluded by advising, "If triplets aren't available, any three teen-agers of the same height would do as well." Fortunately, Elvis had a large enough following that Paramount did not have to rely on these types of stunts to pack the audiences in.

CAST

Ross Carpenter . . . .Elvis Presley
Robin Gantner. . .Stella Stevens
Laurel Dodge . .Laurel Goodwin
Wesley Johnson . . .Jeremy Slate
Chen Yung . . . . . .Guy Lee
Kin Yung . . . . .Benson Fong
Madam Yung. . . .Beulah Quo
Alexander Stavros . . . . . .
. . . . .Frank Puglia
Mama Stavros . . . .Lili Valenty
Sam . . . . . .Robert Strauss
Mai Ling . . . . . .Ginny Tiu
Tai Ling . . . . .Elizabeth Tiu
Baby Brother Ling . . . . . .
. . . . .Alexander Tiu
Mr. Morgan . . . .Nester Paiva
Mrs. Morgan. . . .Ann McCrea
Bongo Player on Tuna Boat . . .
. . . . .Red West
Mr. Peabody . . .Gavin Gordon
Leona Stavros . . .Barbara Beall
Linda Stavros . . . .Betty Beall
Mrs. Dick . . .Marjorie Bennett

CREDITS

Paramount Pictures
Produced by Hal B. Wallis
Directed by Norman Taurog
Screenplay by Edward Anhalt
and Allan Weiss
Photographed in Technicolor by
Loyal Griggs
Music by Joe Lilly
Vocal accompaniment by
The Jordanaires
Choreography by
Charles O'Curran
Released November 21, 1962

Top: *Elvis played a singing boat captain in* Girls! Girls! Girls!, *which was shot in Hawaii.*
Bottom: *In her screen debut, Laurel Goodwin woos and wins Elvis in this light musical comedy.*

THE FILMS OF ELVIS PRESLEY

IT HAPPENED AT
THE WORLD'S FAIR

*Elvis and costar Joan O'Brien
clinch for this magazine
cover promoting the film.*

SONGS

Beyond the Bend

Relax

Take Me to the Fair

They Remind Me Too Much
of You

One Broken Heart for Sale

I'm Falling in Love Tonight

Cotton Candy Land

A World of Our Own

How Would You Like To Be

Happy Ending

STORYLINE

In this musical comedy filmed against the backdrop of the 1963 Seattle World's Fair, Elvis's character, Mike Edwards, and partner Danny Burke, portrayed by Gary Lockwood, hitchhike to Seattle to find work. The two desperately need money to reclaim their airplane, on which the sheriff has attached a lien. They hitch a ride with a Chinese farmer and his seven-year-old niece, Sue-Lin, played by talented Vicky Tiu. When business unexpectedly occupies the uncle, Mike takes Sue-Lin on a tour of the World's Fair, where he meets and falls for nurse Diane Warren, portrayed by Joan O'Brien. When Sue-Lin's uncle fails to return, Mike takes responsibility for the little girl. Mike's situation goes from bad to worse when Child Welfare takes Sue-Lin away and Danny inadvertently becomes involved with a smuggling operation. Mike, Danny, and law officials eventually subdue the smugglers. The film ends happily when Sue-Lin finds her uncle and Mike and Diane find each other.

BEHIND THE SCENES

The transformation of Elvis from rock 'n' roller to handsome leading man that had begun after Elvis's discharge from the Army was complete by *World's Fair*. The change was indicated by the clothes Elvis wore for the film. Newspapers and news magazines ran articles about the specific attire designed for Elvis for the film, but fanzines constructed stories indicating that Elvis had completely changed his mode of dress, both on-screen and off. Sy Devore, a leading Hollywood tailor, was given the job of dressing Elvis for the film. He designed a series of conservative suits and ties to make Elvis "look like a smart, well-dressed young business-man," according to producer Ted Richmond. Devore had to be especially careful about the trousers because Elvis supposedly wore no underwear during this period. The wardrobe, consisting of ten suits, four sports jackets, 30 shirts, 15 pairs of slacks, two cashmere coats, and 55 ties, cost about $10,000.

CAST

Mike Edwards . . .Elvis Presley
Diane Warren . . .Joan O'Brien
Danny Burke . .Gary Lockwood
Sue-Lin . . . . .Vicky Tiu
Vince Bradley. . .H.M. Wynant
Miss Steuben . . .Edith Atwater
Barney Thatcher. . . . . .
. . . . . . .Guy Raymond
Miss Ettinger . .Dorothy Green
Walter Ling . . . . .Kam Tong
Dorothy Johnson . .Yvonne Craig
Sheriff Garland . . . .
. . . . . . .Russell Thorson
Mechanic. . . . .Wilson Wood
Mr. Farr . . .Robert B. Williams
Henry Johnson . . .Olan Soule
Emma Johnson . . . .
. . . . . Jacqueline Dewit
Charlie. . . . . . .John Day
Fred . . . . .Red West
June . . . . . .Sandra Giles
Boy Who Kicks Elvis. . . . .
. . . . .Kurt Russell
Carnival Man. . . .Joe Esposito

CREDITS

Metro-Goldwyn-Mayer

Produced by Ted Richmond

Directed by Norman Taurog

Screenplay by Si Rose
and Seaman Jacobs

Photographed in Metrocolor
and Panavision by
Joseph Ruttenberg

Music by Leith Stevens

Choreography by Jack Baker

Vocal accompaniment by
The Jordanaires
and The Mello Men

Released April 10, 1963

Top: *Gary Lockwood costarred as Elvis's loyal but careless friend and partner.*
Bottom: *During production Elvis dated Yvonne Craig, who had a secondary role in the film.*

THE FILMS OF ELVIS PRESLEY

FUN IN ACAPULCO

This rare photo was taken by a fan during the production of Fun in Acapulco.

STORYLINE

In another version of his musical comedy persona, Elvis stars as Mike Windgren, a former circus performer trying to escape his past. Mike's circus career ended when he caused his partner to be seriously injured during their trapeze act. Traumatized by the accident, Mike has developed a fear of heights. At the beginning of the film, he finds himself in Acapulco, where he hires on as lifeguard at a resort hotel. In the evenings, he entertains the guests by singing. Mike becomes involved with two exotic women—hotel social director Marguerita Dauphin, played by Ursula Andress, and lady bullfighter Dolores Gomez, played by Elsa Cardenas. Mike soon finds himself in competition with another hotel lifeguard, who every night performs a death-defying jump off the ocean cliffs near the hotel. This rival uncovers Mike's past and tricks him into jumping off the cliffs. Ultimately, Mike's decision to jump helps him overcome his fears. He decides to spend his life with Marguerita.

BEHIND THE SCENES

In much of the publicity generated during Elvis's Hollywood career, the press noted that the singer performed many of his own stunts. In *Fun in Acapulco*, Elvis chose to participate in a few stunts that the producers considered risky. In the opening scene, Elvis's character is performing as an aerialist in a circus. The scene called for the character to swing from a high trapeze without a net, 20 feet above the circus floor, and accidentally miss his partner, who plummets to the floor. Every precaution was taken to provide safeguards for Elvis out of camera range, but producer Hal Wallis was still nervous because his star insisted on doing the stunt himself. As a precaution, the studio scheduled the stunt to be performed during the last days of production, when all of Elvis's other scenes had already been filmed. Elvis, who was in top physical condition, performed the stunt without incident. One stunt that Elvis did not do was the thrilling 136-foot dive off the cliffs at La Quebrada, Mexico.

Elvis plants one on Ursula Andress, former James Bond girl and Elvis's hot-blooded costar in Fun in Acapulco.

Mike Windgren . . .Elvis Presley
Marguerita Dauphin . . . . . .
. . . . .Ursula Andress
Dolores Gomez . .Elsa Cardenas
Maximilian Dauphin . . . . .
. . . . .Paul Lukas
Raoul Almeido . .Larry Domasin
Moreno . . . . .Alejandro Rey
Jose Garcia . . .Robert Carricart
Janie Harkins . . . .Teri Hope
Mariachi Los Vaqueros . . . . .
. . . . .Themselves
Mariachi Aguila . . .Themselves
Dr. John Stevers . . . .
. . . . . .Howard McNear
Mr. Ramirez . . .Alberto Morin
Mrs. Stevers. . . . .Mary Treen
Mr. Perez. . . .Salvador Baguez
Mr. Delgado . .Edward Colmans
Mr. Harkins . . .Charles Evans
Guard . . . . . .Mike Deanda
Manager of Tropicana . . . . .
. . . . . .Martin Garralaga
Photographer . .Tom Hernandez
Poolside Guest . . . .Red West

CREDITS

Paramount Pictures

Produced by Hal B. Wallis

Directed by Richard Thorpe

Screenplay by Allan Weiss

Photographed in Technicolor by
Daniel L. Fapp

Music by Joseph J. Lilley

Musical accompaniment by
The Jordanaires

Choreography by
Charles O'Curran

Released November 27, 1963

THE FILMS OF ELVIS PRESLEY

CREDITS

Metro-Goldwyn-Mayer

Produced by Sam Katzman

Directed by Gene Nelson

Screenplay by
Gerald Drayson Adams and
Gene Nelson

Photographed in Metrocolor and
Panavision by Ellis W. Carter

Music by Fred Karger

Released March 6, 1964

Top: *In this lobby card photo, dual Elvises stomp it up with Cynthia Pepper and Yvonne Craig.*
Bottom: *Through special effects, Elvis played an Air Force pilot and his country cousin.*

THE FILMS OF ELVIS PRESLEY

KISSIN' COUSINS

Elvis plays a dual role in this extremely low-budget musical comedy set in the hills of Tennessee but mostly shot on Hollywood sets. As Air Force officer Josh Morgan, a dark-haired Elvis plays a responsible military man; as blond-haired Jodie Tatum, he appears as a girl-chasin', gun-totin' mountain Romeo. Josh is assigned the task of persuading the Tatums, his distant relatives on his mother's side, to sell their land for use as a missile site. When he visits the Tatums, Josh runs into his blond-haired double as well as two beautiful country cousins, Azalea and Selena. The two girls, played by Yvonne Craig and Pam Austin respectively, both vie for Josh's affections. Josh eventually chooses Azalea but not before pairing off Selena with his best friend. In the meantime, Jodie takes up with Midge, a beautiful but fiery WAC played by Cynthia Pepper. Josh persuades Pappy Tatum to sell one side of his mountain to the government as long as the military does not interfere with Pappy's moonshining on the other side.

Yvonne Craig and Pamela Austin look admiringly at a blond-wigged Elvis. Oddly enough, the wig was quite close to his true hair color.

BEHIND THE SCENES

Kissin' Cousins, produced by Sam Katzman, is consistently singled out as Elvis's worst film. Katzman had a notorious reputation for churning out low-budget films on short schedules. Estimates on how long it took to shoot *Kissin' Cousins* vary from source to source, but all claim it was less than three weeks. The film was budgeted at $800,000, compared with the $4 million budget of *Blue Hawaii*.

To help control expenses, the songs were written in assembly-line fashion. Katzman decided that since the film had a "country" theme, the songs should be recorded in Nashville rather than Hollywood, where all Elvis's previous soundtrack albums had been recorded. However, these mediocre tunes were only some songwriting hack's misguided interpretation of what country-and-western music was like. The eight songs in the film, including "Barefoot Ballad," "Pappy, Won't You

Kissin' Cousins

Smokey Mountain Boy

One Boy, Two Little Girls

Catchin' on Fast

Tender Feeling

Barefoot Ballad

Once Is Enough

Kissin' Cousins (reprise)

Pappy, Won't You Please
Come Home
(sung by Farrell's character)

Please Come Home," and the title tune, sounded nothing like the country music of the era.

The few exterior shots for the film were done at Big Bear Lake in California. When the location shooting was finished, Elvis was involved in what could have been a fatal accident. While driving down the mountain from Big Bear Lake in a mobile home, Elvis was shocked when the brakes on the vehicle completely gave out. A car carrying some of the film crew was traveling ahead of the huge vehicle lumbering down the mountain. The road was too narrow for Elvis to pass the car, and a sheer drop on one side made the speed they were traveling at quite dangerous. Elvis had to use the gears to maneuver down the mountain, while the car managed to stay just ahead of them. When the mobile home reached the bottom of the mountain, Elvis kept the vehicle running until it eventually slowed to a stop. Had Elvis not been such a competent driver, *Kissin' Cousins* would have been his legacy to his fans.

Kissin' Cousins marked a change in approach toward making Elvis's films. It seemed to set a pattern in which the shooting schedules grew shorter and the budgets got lower. Some argue that Colonel Parker realized that Elvis's popularity was starting to wane, so he began seeking out producers who could lower production costs, as well as seeking out resorts and hotels that would allow the casts and crews to stay for free. There is no actual proof of this. Perhaps the reverse was true. The decline in production values accompanying lower budgets and shorter schedules could have contributed to the decline in box-office receipts.

Elvis checks his coif while Pamela Austin and Yvonne Craig take a breather between scenes.

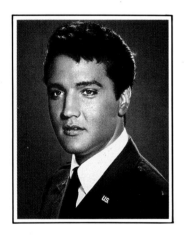

One-half of Elvis's dual role was as Air Force pilot Josh Morgan.

The military people enjoy country music as much as the locals.

THE FILMS OF ELVIS PRESLEY

Sam Katzman's films were long on corny musical numbers but short on production values.

SAM KATZMAN

Sam Katzman entered the film industry at the tender age of 13 when he began work as a prop boy. Eventually, he worked his way up through various studio positions to became a producer. His reputation for producing low-budget films is so prevalent that he has been nicknamed "The King of the Quickies." In his prime, Katzman aimed particularly at the action and juvenile markets.

Left, top: *Elvis, Glenda Farrell, W.J. (Sailor) Vincent, and Arthur O'Connell meet over a table filled with country-cooked vittles. Left, bottom: Cynthia Pepper decks Elvis flat in this original lobby card from* Kissin' Cousins.

CAST

Lucky Jackson . . .Elvis Presley
Rusty Martin . . .Ann Margret
Count Elmo Mancini. . . . . .
. . . . . . .Cesare Danova
Mr. Martin . .William Demarest
Shorty Farnsworth . .Nicky Blair
Jack Carter . . . . .Himself
Mr. Swanson . . . .
. . . . .Robert B. Williams
Big Gus Olson . . . .Bob Nash
Mr. Baker . . . . . .Roy Engel
Mechanic. . . .Barnaby Hale
Driver . . . . .Ford Dunhill
Master of Ceremonies . . . . .
. . . . .Eddie Quillan
Manager at Swingers. . . . . .
. . . . .George Cisar
Delivery boy . . . .Rick Murray
The Forte Four . . .Themselves
Showgirls . . .Aleane Mambi
Hamilton, Beverly Powers, Kay
Sutton, Ingeborg Kjeldsen, Teri
Garr

CREDITS

Metro-Goldwyn-Mayer

Produced by Jack Cummings and
George Sidney

Directed by George Sidney

Screenplay by Sally Benson

Photographed in Metrocolor by
Joseph Biroc

Music by George Stoll

Choreography by David Winters

Released June 17, 1964

*Ann-Margret races near the Las Vegas airport with Elvis in hot pursuit. The two scared the producers
of* Viva Las Vegas *half to death by racing their motorcycles offscreen as well.*

VIVA LAS VEGAS

In *Viva Las Vegas*, perhaps his best musical comedy, Elvis was finally teamed with a costar whose singing and dancing matched the intensity of his own performing style. As Rusty Martin, dynamic Ann-Margret perfectly complemented Elvis's character of Lucky Jackson. Lucky, a race-car driver whose car desperately needs a new engine, arrives in Las Vegas for the Vegas Grand Prix. He and fellow driver Count Elmo Mancini, played by Cesare Danova, are rivals on the track as well as off the track, competing for the affections of Rusty. Rusty works at the same hotel as Lucky, who throughout the film is trying to raise money to fix his car. Rusty is reluctant to become seriously involved with Lucky because of the dangers of his occupation. Eventually, she changes her mind and assists him in his last-minute efforts to complete his repairs. Lucky lives up to his name and wins the Grand Prix.

B E H I N D   T H E   S C E N E S

Elvis was not restricted to working only for Hal Wallis and Paramount, since the contract he signed with them was not an exclusive one. Elvis also worked for other producers at other studios, including MGM, United Artists, and Allied Artists. Interestingly, the producers from these other studios tended to follow the musical comedy formula that Wallis had developed for Elvis, and occasionally even improving on it. Though *Viva Las Vegas* follows the familiar formula of the "Presley travelogue," the inclusion of dynamic Ann-Margret made it a cut above the rest. Shot predominantly in Las Vegas, the film made effective use of such locations as the Flamingo and Tropicana hotels and the drag strip at Henderson, Nevada.

Viva Las Vegas is perhaps best remembered for the romance between Elvis Presley and Ann-Margret. The romance was played out on the front pages of the newspapers after the two were noticed attending restaurants and nightclubs together in Las Vegas. The publicity surrounding the

Ann-Margret sings songs from Viva Las Vegas *on this autographed album.*

S O N G S

Viva Las Vegas

The Yellow Rose of Texas

The Lady Loves Me

C'mon Everybody

Today, Tomorrow and Forever

What'd I Say

Santa Lucia

If You Think I Don't Love You

I Need Somebody to Lean On

My Rival
(sung by Ann-Margret's character)

Appreciation
(sung by Ann-Margret's character)

The Climb
(sung by The Forte Four)

romance was a dream come true for the producers of *Viva Las Vegas*. Even Elvis's hometown newspaper, the *Memphis Press-Scimitar*, ran stories with such sensational headlines as "It Looks Like Romance for Elvis and Ann-Margret" and "Elvis Wins Love of Ann-Margret."

Ironically, Elvis was not happy at first to be teamed with Ann-Margret, although he was flattered that she was known as "the female Elvis Presley." Supposedly, someone on the production team of *Viva Las Vegas* had dated her during an earlier film venture and was still smitten by her charm and beauty. This crew member assisted with the photography on *Viva Las Vegas* and seemed to favor Ann-Margret with better lighting and camera angles. When Elvis complained to the Colonel, the big guns came to the rescue and the crew member was soon chastised. Elvis ultimately realized it was not the fault of Ann-Margret, and the two young performers quickly grew close. The obvious chemistry between them was an asset to their performances on-screen. The two generated an electricity during their musical numbers seldom matched in Elvis's later films.

Ann-Margret shared many things in common with Elvis, including the pressures of a show business career. Both enjoyed similar activities, such as riding motorcycles, and she got along well with Elvis's group of buddy-bodyguards. They called her "Rusty Ammo," or "Ann-Margrock."

The romance between these two high-profile stars did not survive the production of the film. Rumors abound as to what split them up, ranging from Elvis's relationship with Priscilla Beaulieu to Ann-Margret's hasty confession to the press that she and Elvis were engaged. Though the relationship did not work out in the long term, Elvis and Ann-Margret remained friends for the rest of his life. Elvis would later marry Priscilla Beaulieu, and Ann-Margret would marry actor Roger Smith. According to Ann-Margret, Elvis sent her flowers in the shape of a guitar on the opening night of every one of her Las Vegas engagements.

Elvis starred as race car driver Lucky Jackson in Viva Las Vegas. *Racing cars was a typical occupation for the characters Elvis played in the movies.*

Elvis and Ann-Margret team up for a dynamic rendition of "C'mon Everybody."

ANN-MARGRET

Born Ann-Margret Olson in Stockholm, Ann-Margret emigrated to the United States when she was seven. Her first film role was as Bette Davis's daughter in Pocketful of Miracles *in 1961, but it wasn't until 1963's* Bye, Bye Birdie *that she was recognized as a powerful entertainer.* Bye, Bye Birdie— *about a famous rock singer going off to the service—was loosely based on the controversy and phenomenon caused by Elvis in 1958. It seemed to be fate that Ann-Margret should appear with Elvis in her very next film. Her role in* Carnal Knowledge *not only indicated her range as a serious actress but also garnered her an Oscar nomination.*

The chemistry between Elvis and Ann-Margret is readily apparent even in the publicity stills.

ROUSTABOUT

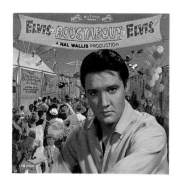

The soundtrack album for Roustabout *was number one on the pop charts for a week.*

S T O R Y L I N E

Playing opposite Barbara Stanwyck this time out, Elvis was in awe of his costar and worked hard to live up to her professional standards. Unfortunately, the scriptwriters were less demanding of themselves, and the film suffers from banal dialogue and predictable plotting. Elvis stars as Charlie Rogers, a drifter with a chip on his shoulder who lands a job as a roustabout, or handyman, with a down-and-out carnival operated by strong-willed Maggie Morgan, played by Stanwyck. When Charlie breaks into song on the midway one day, throngs of young people flock to hear him sing. As news of his talent spreads, Maggie's carnival begins to turn a tidy profit. Charlie's good fortune continues as Cathy, a beautiful young carnival worker played by Joan Freeman, takes a romantic interest in him. However, after a misunderstanding involving a customer's missing wallet, Maggie and Cathy chide Charlie for his selfish attitudes. The embittered young man quits Maggie's outfit to work for a rival carnival. When Maggie's carnival starts to go under, Charlie returns with enough money to ward off the creditors. His unselfish act wins Maggie's respect as well as Cathy's heart.

B E H I N D   T H E   S C E N E S

A cast of big-name stars, including Barbara Stanwyck, Leif Erickson, and Jack Albertson, made *Roustabout* one of Elvis's best vehicles. Wallis's solid reputation in Hollywood often helped secure some of the bigger names for Elvis's movies, and this film was no exception. Supposedly, Mae West was first approached for Stanwyck's role but declined the offer. The combination of Elvis Presley and Mae West would have made a sensational screen pairing. Stanwyck's image as a tough, independent woman suited the character. Edith Head, Hollywood's most illustrious costume designer, did the clothing for the film, even designing a special pair of formfitting jeans for Stanwyck. Elvis would later say that working with Stanwyck made him a better actor.

CAST

Charlie Rogers . . . .Elvis Presley
Maggie Morgan . . . .
. . . . . .Barbara Stanwyck
Cathy Lean . . . .Joan Freeman
Joe Lean . . . . .Leif Erickson
Madame Mijanou . . . .
. . . . . .Sue Ane Langdon
Harry Carver . . . .Pat Buttram
Marge . . . . . .Joan Staley
Arthur Nielsen. . .Dabbs Greer
Freddie . . . . .Steve Brodie
Sam, A College Student. . . .
. . . . .Norman Grabowski
Lou . . . . . .Jack Albertson
Hazel . . . . . . .Jane Dulo
Cody Marsh . . . .Joe Fluellen
Billy . . . . .Billy Barty
Little Egypt . . . .Wilda Taylor
Viola . . . . . .Marianna Hill
Strong Man . . . .Richard Kiel
Carnival Worker . . .Red West
College Student . .Raquel Welch

CREDITS

Paramount Pictures
Produced by Hal B. Wallis
Directed by John Rich
Screenplay by Anthony Lawrence
and Allan Weiss
Photographed in Technicolor and
Techniscope by Lucien Ballard
Music by Joseph L. Lilley
Vocal accompaniment by
The Jordanaires
Released November 11, 1964

Top: *Barbara Stanwyck and Elvis meet on the carnival midway.* Bottom: *Elvis tries to charm costar Joan Freeman with his various "talents," but she remains aloof.*

THE FILMS OF ELVIS PRESLEY

Top: *Elvis once said that Shelley Fabares was his favorite costar.* Bottom: *This original lobby card shows (from left) Elvis, Jimmy Hawkins, Gary Crosby, and Joby Baker.*

GIRL HAPPY

To take advantage of the popularity among college students of the Ft. Lauderdale Easter vacation, producer Joe Pasternak put together this youth-oriented flick combining Elvis Presley, Ft. Lauderdale, bikini-clad girls, and wacky dance crazes. Elvis stars as struggling pop singer Rusty Wells, whose musical combo works for a tough Chicago nightclub owner known as Big Frank. Big Frank's big weakness is his only daughter Valerie, who insists on spending her Easter vacation in sunny, sinful Ft. Lauderdale. Frank sends Rusty and his friends to Florida to keep an eye on Valerie without her knowing about it. Rusty attempts to pursue a few college coeds of his own, but he is constantly interrupted by the need to rescue Valerie from various Ft. Lauderdale loverboys. Naturally, Valerie, played by Shelley Fabares in her first Elvis Presley musical, falls in love with the smooth-talking Rusty.

BEHIND THE SCENES

After working on several musical vehicles back-to-back, Elvis began to tire of the same type of role over and over. He also complained of the endless succession of mediocre pop tunes that filled each soundtrack. Sensing his disillusionment, director Boris Sagal took Elvis aside and urged him to stop his grueling film schedule. Sagal suggested that Elvis take time off to study acting in New York, perhaps at the acclaimed Actors Studio or the famous Neighborhood Playhouse. The director supposedly told Elvis, "Every actor studies his trade, even those as good as Marlon Brando." Elvis agreed, admitting that he looked forward to the day when he could do a film without any music. But *Girl Happy* would not be that film. This lively but formulaic spring vacation comedy contained 11 songs for Elvis—about average for a Presley picture.

Girl Happy featured some familiar faces from other youth-oriented films, including Joby Baker, Jimmy Hawkins, and Gary Crosby as Elvis's wacky musical trio. Of the three actors, only Crosby (the son of Bing

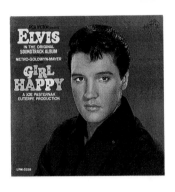

"Girl Happy" remained on Billboard's Top LPs chart for 31 weeks, peaking at number eight.

SONGS

Girl Happy

Spring Fever

Fort Lauderdale Chamber of Commerce

Startin' Tonight

Wolf Call

Do Not Disturb

Cross My Heart and Hope to Die

The Meanest Girl in Town

Do the Clam

Puppet on a String

I've Got to Find My Baby

Read All About It (sung by Talbot's and Fabares's characters)

Crosby) had any musical talent. The film also costarred television actress Shelley Fabares, whose popularity with audiences was undoubtedly the result of her role as the eldest daughter on *The Donna Reed Show*. No stranger to the pop music scene, she had recorded "Johnny Angel," a number-one hit in 1962. Her role opposite Elvis in *Girl Happy* proved quite successful, and she costarred in two subsequent Presley films, *Spinout* and *Clambake*. Elvis later declared her to be his favorite costar.

Of the dozen or so tunes in *Girl Happy*, two are particularly memorable—the low-down and bluesy "Wolf Call" and the easy-sounding ballad "Puppet on a String." One song in the film is frequently mentioned as one of the worst tunes ever recorded by Elvis, though he should not have to shoulder the blame. "Do the Clam" was written as accompaniment for a dance called the clam that was specially created for the film by choreographer David Winters. Winters, the dance director for the rock 'n' roll TV program *Hullabaloo*, had also choreographed *Viva Las Vegas*. He was quite familiar with modern music, but the clam never caught on. During the mid-1960s, several dance crazes swept the nation, including the monkey, the pony, the swim, and countless others. Though the clam was not the success the film's producers hoped it would be, it nonetheless reflected the era. When put in the context of the times, the song and the dance are not nearly so outrageous.

Elvis croons "Ft. Lauderdale Chamber of Commerce" to Shelley Fabares in a scene from a lobby card.

Shelley and Elvis collapse after doing the clam at a beach party. The clam was a new dance created for the film by pop choreographer David Winters.

Elvis and his combo perform for a laid-back Ft. Lauderdale crowd.

This behind-the-scenes candid captures (from left) Nita Talbot, Shelley Fabares, Elvis, and Mary Ann Mobley.

Left, top: *Though Crosby (left), Hawkins (right), and Baker (on drums) play Elvis's backup musicians, only Crosby—the son of singing legend Bing Crosby—had any musical experience.*
Left, bottom: *As Police Sergeant Benson, Jackie Coogan bawls out Elvis and his combo. A renowned character actor, Coogan had been appearing in films since he was 18 months old.*

TICKLE ME

Tickle Me saved Allied Artists from financial disaster. It was the third-highest grossing film in the studio's history.

SONGS

Long, Lonely Highway

It Feels So Right

(Such an) Easy Question

Dirty, Dirty Feeling

Put the Blame on Me

I'm Yours

Night Rider

I Feel That I've Known
You Before

Slowly but Surely

Elvis and Jocelyn Lane pose for a publicity still.

STORYLINE

By *Tickle Me*, the storylines of Elvis's musicals had become paper-thin and the credibility of his characters had become strained by their ridiculous occupations. Though disturbing to critics and biographers, fans understand that the appeal is Elvis himself, not his characters. Here, Elvis stars as Lonnie Beale, a singing rodeo cowboy who moonlights as a handyman at a beauty spa. Though several women try to catch the attention of Lonnie, including spa owner Vera Radford, played by Julie Adams, the rodeo rider falls for Pam Merritt. Pam, portrayed by Jocelyn Lane, is visiting the spa to investigate a nearby ghost town where her grandfather has supposedly hidden a cache of gold. Pam enlists the help of Lonnie and his sidekick Stanley, played by Jack Mullaney, to recover the treasure. Unscrupulous locals, also looking for the gold, try to frighten the hapless trio into leaving the territory, but the three eventually prevail. Lonnie and Pam marry at the end, marking one of the few times that one of Elvis's characters actually weds on-screen.

BEHIND THE SCENES

Tickle Me represented a somewhat different arrangement between Colonel Parker, Elvis, and Allied Artists Productions, the studio producing the film. Allied was facing deep financial trouble. They desperately wanted to make a deal with Elvis because a Presley picture was a guaranteed money-maker. The Colonel agreed to cut Elvis's salary from $1 million to $750,000 (plus the usual 50 percent of the profits) to help Allied cut expenses. This meant that the studio had to come up with the rest of the budget—a mere $750,000. To keep within that minuscule budget, no new songs were purchased or recorded for the film. The soundtrack was made up of previously recorded Elvis tunes. True to form, this Elvis musical comedy was financially successful. Allied executive Steve Brody later admitted Elvis's hand in saving his studio, "You might say they were ready to wheel the patient out when Dr. Presley came in."

CAST

Lonnie Beale	.Elvis Presley
Vera Radford . . .	.Julie Adams
Pam Merritt . . .	.Jocelyn Lane
Stanley Potter . .	.Jack Mullaney
Estelle Penfield .	.Merry Anders
Deputy John Sturdivant	
. . . .	.Bill Williams
Brad Bentley .	.Edward Faulkner
Hilda	.Connie Gilchrist
Barbara	.Barbara Werle
Adolph the Chef .	.John Dennis
Mr. Dabney . . .	.Grady Sutton
Mabel	.Allison Hayes
Ophelia	.Inez Pedroza
Ronnie	.Lilyan Chauvin
Donna	.Angela Greene
Henry the Gardener	
. . . .	.Robert Hoy
Mrs. Dabney .	.Dorothy Konrad
Pat	.Eve Bruce
Mildred	.Francine York
Bully in Bar	.Red West

CREDITS

Allied Artists Productions

Produced by Ben Schwalb

Directed by Norman Taurog

Screenplay by Elwood Ullman
and Edward Bernds

Photographed in DeLuxe Color
and Panavision by Loyal Griggs

Music by Walter Scharf

Vocal accompaniment by
The Jordanaires

Choreography by David Winters

Released May 28, 1965

Top: *As singing rodeo rider Lonnie Beale, Elvis serenades a bevy of beauties.* Bottom: *Elvis and costar Jocelyn Lane. In 1971, Lane became a princess when she married into royalty.*

THE FILMS OF ELVIS PRESLEY

HARUM SCARUM

The soundtrack album had 11 songs, two more than the film.

SONGS

Harem Holiday

My Desert Serenade

Go East, Young Man

Mirage

Kismet

Shake That Tambourine

Hey, Little Girl

Golden Coins

So Close,
Yet So Far (from Paradise)

Elvis and Mary Ann Mobley listen to a scheme by Jay Novello.

STORYLINE

Another "quickie" produced on a very low budget by Sam Katzman, *Harum Scarum* features Elvis as matinee idol Johnny Tyronne. A takeoff on Elvis himself, Johnny is a famous movie and recording star who makes the women swoon and the men jealous. On a personal appearance tour in Lunarkand—a fictional country somewhere in the Middle East—Johnny is kidnapped by a gang of assassins and suddenly thrust into a plot to kill King Toranshah. Johnny escapes and falls in with a band of pickpockets and rogues, all the while rescuing damsels in distress and singing a variety of pop-styled tunes. Johnny falls in love with a beautiful handmaiden, played by Mary Ann Mobley; unbeknownst to him, she is really Princess Shalimar, daughter of King Toranshah. Johnny thwarts the assassination attempt on the king, wins the heart of Princess Shalimar, and returns to America with a new act. He opens in Las Vegas with a Middle Eastern dancing troupe, complete with exotic harem girls.

BEHIND THE SCENES

With a shooting schedule of only 18 days, *Harum Scarum* was a no-frills production with little time or money to spend on props, costumes, or set design. Little if anything was actually purchased or designed for the film, a not uncommon practice for low-budget productions. The temple set had originally been built in 1925 for a Cecil B. DeMille silent feature called *King of Kings*. The costumes worn by the extras in *Harum Scarum* had been used in the 1944 version of *Kismet* and then retailored for the 1955 musical remake. Even the dagger carried by Elvis had been used in an earlier adventure film, *Lady of the Tropics*. Little effort was invested in the script, and the plot was thrown together following the same Presley formula. How bad was it? The Colonel suggested adding a talking camel to the storyline, which was seriously considered for a time before it was mercifully dropped.

CAST

Johnny Tyronne . . .Elvis Presley
Princess Shalimar . . . . . .
. . . . . .Mary Ann Mobley
Aishah . . . . .Fran Jeffries
Prince Dragna . .Michael Ansara
Zacha . . . . . .Jay Novello
King Toranshah . . .Philip Reed
Sinan . . . . .Theo Marcuse
Baba . . . . . . .Billy Barty
Mokar . . . . .Dick Harvey
Julna. . . . . .Jack Costanza
Captain Herat . . .Larry Chance
Leilah . . . . .Barbara Werle
Emerald . . . .Brenda Benet
Sapphire . . . .Gail Gilmore
Amethyst . . . .Wilda Taylor
Sari . . . . . . .Vicki Malkin
Mustapha . . . .Ryck Rydon
Scarred Bedouin. . . . . . .
. . . . . . .Richard Reeves
Yussef . . . . . .Joey Russo
Assassin . . . . . .Red West

CREDITS

Metro-Goldwyn-Mayer
Produced by Sam Katzman
Directed by Gene Nelson
Screenplay by
Gerald Drayson Adams
Photographed in Metrocolor by
Fred H. Jackman
Music by Fred Karger
Vocal accompaniment by
The Jordanaires
Released November 24, 1965

Top: *Elvis croons "Mirage" to a harem of slave girls in the Garden of Paradise.*
Bottom: *Elvis sings about his "Harem Holiday" in the rousing finale.*

THE FILMS OF ELVIS PRESLEY

FRANKIE AND JOHNNY

A color photograph of Elvis was included as a bonus in the soundtrack album.

SONGS

Come Along

Petunia,
the Gardener's Daughter

Chesay

What Every Woman Lives For

Frankie and Johnny

Look Out, Broadway

Beginner's Luck

Down by the Riverside/
When the Saints Go Marching In

Shout It Out

Hard Luck

Please Don't Stop Loving Me

Everybody Come Aboard

STORYLINE

In a slight change of pace, Elvis appeared in this lighthearted musical based on the folk song, "Frankie and Johnny." In the original song, the title characters are lovers whose romance goes awry when red-headed Nellie Bly steals Johnny away from Frankie. Frankie gets revenge by shooting Johnny dead. The movie lightens the tone of the tale by adding a few details and changing the downbeat ending. In the film, the song has been specially written for riverboat performers Frankie and Johnny, played by Donna Douglas and Elvis. Johnny is a gambler whose bad luck changes when dancer Nellie Bly, played by Nancy Kovack, joins the troupe aboard the riverboat. Each night, the three perform the number "Frankie and Johnny" onstage. As Johnny's interest in Nellie increases, Frankie's jealousy is piqued. One night, someone loads real bullets into Frankie's prop gun, and Johnny is shot during the performance. As luck would have it, Johnny is saved by a charm that he wears around his neck.

BEHIND THE SCENES

One of the few period pieces Elvis starred in during his film career, *Frankie and Johnny* was set during the Victorian Era and made full use of its colorful costumes and riverboat setting. The reviews were mixed regarding the film: Some critics felt the setting was a welcome change for a Presley picture, while others recognized the same old storyline under the period costumes. Despite the nay-sayers, the film benefited from the juicy secondary roles played by a seasoned cast of character actors. Harry Morgan, who later gained recognition on the TV series *M*A*S*H*, played Cully the piano player. Sue Ane Langdon portrayed Mitzi, the girl who is always edged out in the romance department. It was the type of role that had become Langdon's specialty. Robert Strauss, the burly villain in many crime dramas, played Blackie, the boss's stooge. Directed by Frederick de Cordova, who later became the director of *The Tonight Show*, the film is notable for its good production values.

CAST

Johnny . . . . . .Elvis Presley
Frankie. . . . .Donna Douglas
Cully . . . . . .Harry Morgan
Mitzi . . . . .Sue Ane Langdon
Nellie Bly . . . .Nancy Kovack
Peg . . . . . .Audrey Christie
Blackie . . . . .Robert Strauss
Braden . . . . .Anthony Eisley
Abigail . . . . .Joyce Jameson
Joe Wilbur . . .Jerome Cowan
Proprietor of Costume Shop. . .
. . . . . . .James Milhollin
Princess Zolita . .Naomi Stevens
Gypsy . . . . . .Henry Corden
Pete the Bartender. . . . . .
. . . . .Dave Willock
Man on the Street . . . . . .
. . . . . .Richard J. Reeves
Bit. . . . . . .George Klein

CREDITS

United Artists

Produced by Edward Small

Directed by
Frederick de Cordova

Screenplay by Alex Gottlieb

Based on a story by Nat Perrin

Photographed in Technicolor
by Jacques Marquette

Music by Fred Karger

Vocal accompaniment by
The Jordanaires

Released March 31, 1966

Top: *The storyline for* Frankie and Johnny *was based on the old 19th-century folk song.*
Bottom: *Elvis pleads to Donna Douglas to "Please Don't Stop Loving Me" in a passionate ballad.*

PARADISE, HAWAIIAN STYLE

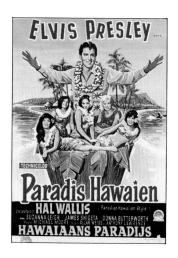

This French movie poster emphasizes the film's tropical setting.

SONGS

Paradise, Hawaiian Style

Queenie Wahini's Papaya

Scratch My Back (Then I'll Scratch Yours)

Drums of the Islands

A Dog's Life

Datin'

House of Sand

Stop Where You Are

This Is My Heaven

Bill Bailey, Won't You Please Come Home (sung by Butterworth's character)

STORYLINE

Elvis's third film based in Hawaii features the singer as Greg "Rick" Richards, a helicopter pilot who starts a charter service with his friend Danny, played by James Shigeta. Rick has coaxed three beautiful women employed at various tourist-related businesses around the Islands to steer customers to their helicopter service. Covering the office is beautiful Judy Hudson, played by Suzanna Leigh, whom Rick and Danny call "Friday." Danny fears that Rick will not be able to resist Judy so he tells the island Romeo that their girl "Friday" is married. A misunderstanding involving a forced helicopter landing results in Rick having his license temporarily suspended. Under orders from the Federal Aviation Agency (FAA) not to fly, Rick risks his license to rescue Danny and his daughter from a deserted island. The FAA understands the mitigating circumstances surrounding Rick's decision and assures him he will be able to fly again. In the meantime, Rick discovers that Judy is not married, and the two embark on romance.

BEHIND THE SCENES

Elvis became notorious for romancing the female costars of his films. From Tuesday Weld and Ann-Margret to such lesser-known starlets as Yvonne Craig and Joan O'Brien, Elvis often swept his costars off their feet both on the screen and off. One actress who was not impressed with Elvis, either professionally or personally, was Marianna Hill, who gained attention as Elvis's partner in the "Scratch My Back" number from *Paradise, Hawaiian Style*. According to press interviews at the time, Hill was annoyed with members of Elvis's management team who kept asking the skeptical actress, "Hasn't Elvis got talent?" Always honest but diplomatic, Hill managed to reply that she thought he was "a show business phenomenon." When asked if she would date Elvis, she replied, "No," citing the singer's ever-present staff of bodyguards and pals as a bit odd.

CAST

Greg "Rick" Richards . . . . .
. . . . .Elvis Presley
Judy Hudson . . .Suzanna Leigh
Danny Kohana . .James Shigeta
Jan Kohana. . . . .
. . . . .Donna Butterworth
Lani Kaimana . .Marianna Hill
Pua . . . . .Irene Tsu
Lehua Kawena . . .Linda Wong
Joanna . . . . . .Julie Parrish
Betty Kohana. . . .Jan Shepard
Donald Belden . .John Doucette
Moke Kaimana . . .Philip Ahn
Mr. Cubberson. . .Grady Sutton
Andy Lowell . . . .Dan Collier
Mrs. Daisy Barrington . . . . .
. . . . .Doris Packer
Mrs. Belden . . . .Mary Treen
Peggy . . . . . .Gi Gi Verone
Dancer. . . . . .Edy Williams
Rusty . . . . . . .Red West

CREDITS

Paramount Pictures

Produced by Hal B. Wallis

Directed by Michael Moore

Screenplay by Allan Weiss and
Anthony Lawrence

Photographed in Technicolor by
W. Wallace Kelley

Music by Joseph J. Lilley

Vocal accompaniment by
The Jordanaires

Released July 6, 1966

Top: *Elvis reprises a dramatic rendition of "Drums of the Islands" during the colorful finale.*
Bottom: *Elvis and young costar Donna Butterworth share an adventure on a small deserted island.*

THE FILMS OF ELVIS PRESLEY

SPINOUT

Elvis played a race car driver in this breezy comedy.

Elvis and his real-life buddies wait for the next scene.

STORYLINE

Playing a singing race-car driver once again, Elvis stars as dashing Mike McCoy. Mike fronts a popular singing group, and he is also the defending champion on the racing circuit. Fast cars are not nearly as dangerous for Mike as beautiful women, all of whom want to race him down the aisle to marriage. Les, played by perky Deborah Walley, works as the drummer in Mike's band, and she is extremely jealous of his attention toward other women. Also vying for Mike's affection is sophisticated Cynthia Foxhugh, played by Shelley Fabares, who is the daughter of wealthy auto magnate Howard Foxhugh. Finally, representing the intellectual type is writer Diana St. Clair, played by Diane McBain, who falls in love with Mike while finishing her book *The Perfect American Male*. In an ending that seems to mock Elvis films in general, Mike does not end up marrying any of these women. Instead, he succeeds in wedding them to friends and associates, while he remains free to begin a new romance.

BEHIND THE SCENES

The story of how *Spinout* came to be proves that Elvis's movies were perceived by Hollywood as lightweight vehicles that could be churned out cheaply and quickly. The scriptwriters for *Spinout*, George Kirgo and Theodore Flicker, had originally been commissioned to write a script for Sonny and Cher. Shortly thereafter, they received a call from MGM to write something for Elvis instead. They quickly finished the script and showed it to the Colonel, who declared that he loved it. Just one thing, though. Could they put a dog in it? Kirgo and Flicker accommodated the Colonel, only to be summoned by the producers a few days later. Could they put a race car in it? Again, they obliged, though it changed the focus of their original idea, which had been to do a romantic farce. Their title for the film—*After Midnight*—was quickly dumped by MGM in favor of *Never Say No*, and then *Never Say Yes*. Finally, Kirgo suggested *Spinout*, which was the discarded title of another script he had written earlier.

CAST

Mike McCoy . . . . .Elvis Presley
Cynthia Foxhugh
. . . . .Shelley Fabares
Diana St. Clair . .Diane McBain
Les . . . . . .Deborah Walley
Susan. . . . . .Dodie Marshall
Curly . . . . . .Jack Mullaney
Lt. Tracy Richards . . . . . .
. . . . .Will Hutchins
Philip Short . .Warren Berlinger
Larry. . . . . .Jimmy Hawkins
Howard Foxhugh . . .Carl Betz
Bernard Ranley . .Cecil Kellaway
Violet Ranley . . . .Una Merkel
Blodgett . . . .Frederic Worlock
Harry . . . . . . .Dave Barry
Race Announcer . . .Jay Jasin
Shorty Bloomquist. . . . . . .
. . . . . . .James McHale
Shorty's Pit Crew . . . .
. . .Red West and Joe Esposito

CREDITS

Metro-Goldwyn-Mayer

Produced by Joe Pasternak

Directed by Norman Taurog

Screenplay by George Kirgo and
Theodore Flicker

Photograped in Metrocolor by
Daniel L. Fapp

Music by George Stoll

Vocal accompaniment by
The Jordanaires

Released November 23, 1966

Top: *Elvis costarred with three actresses in* Spinout, *including Deborah Walley.* Bottom: *(from left)*
Shelley Fabares, Deborah Walley, and Diane McBain vie for Elvis's hand in marriage.

THE FILMS OF ELVIS PRESLEY

EASY COME, EASY GO

Character actress Elsa Lanchester (top) was featured in a secondary role as yoga instructor Madame Neherina.

SONGS

Easy Come, Easy Go

The Love Machine

Yoga Is as Yoga Does

You Gotta Stop

Sing, You Children

I'll Take Love

Elvis and Dodie Marshall. Earlier titles for the film included Port of Call, A Girl in Every Port, Nice and Easy, and Easy Does It.

STORYLINE

In his last film for Hal Wallis, Elvis stars as Navy frogman Ted Jackson, who is about to be discharged from the service. On one of his last dives, Ted discovers a treasure chest on a sunken ship. Captain Jack, a local expert on nautical lore, is unable to tell Ted the exact treasure or cargo of the ship. But Captain Jack does reveal the name of the only descendant of the ship's captain. Ted tracks down this descendant—a vivacious young woman named Jo Symington, played by Dodie Marshall. Jo believes the chest contains pieces-of-eight. She agrees to help Ted if the money is given to the community arts center. Their attempts to retrieve the treasure are impeded by scoundrels Gil Carey and Dina Bishop. Carey and Bishop steal Ted's equipment and kidnap Captain Jack, but Ted tracks them down and rescues Jack. When Ted opens the chest, he discovers that the coins are copper, not gold. Ted donates the money for a down payment on a new arts center, winning Jo in the process.

BEHIND THE SCENES

Elvis usually got along well with his directors; the exception was John Rich, who directed Elvis in *Roustabout* and *Easy Come, Easy Go.* More a television director than a film director, Rich managed to snag some big-screen assignments during the mid-1960s. His film work tended to be glossy but uninspired. Rich and Elvis did not get along on the set of *Roustabout,* and their mutual feelings of animosity did not disappear by the time cameras rolled on *Easy Come, Easy Go.* One afternoon, Elvis and Red West were trying to do a scene together but were hampered by a case of the giggles. Angered by what he felt was unprofessional behavior, Rich threw all of Elvis's buddy-bodyguards off the set. Elvis was furious. He put everything into perspective for Rich and the film's producers when he frankly told them, "Now, just a minute. We're doing these movies because it's supposed to be fun, nothing more. Now when they cease to be fun, then we'll cease to do them." If that had only been the case. . . .

CAST

Ted Jackson . . . .Elvis Presley
Jo Symington . .Dodie Marshall
Dina Bishop . . . . .Pat Priest
Judd Whitman . . . .
. . . . . .Pat Harrington, Jr.
Gil Carey . . . . . .Skip Ward
Madame Neherina. . . . . .
. . . . . . .Elsa Lanchester
Captain Jack. . .Frank McHugh
Lt. Marty Schwartz. . . . . .
. . . . .Sandy Kenyon
Cooper. . . . . . .Ed Griffith
Lieutenant Tompkins. . . . .
. . . . .Reed Morgan
Lieutenant Whitehead . . . . .
. . . . .Mickey Elley
Vicki . . . . . .Elaine Beckett
Mary . . . . . . .Shari Nims
Zoltan . . . . . . .Diki Lerner
Tanya . . . . .Kay York
Artist . . . . .Robert Isenberg
Naval Officer . . . .Tom Hatten
Coin Dealer . . .Jonathan Hole

CREDITS

Paramount Pictures

Produced by Hal B. Wallis

Directed by John Rich

Screenplay by Allan Weiss and
Anthony Lawrence

Photographed in Technicolor by
William Margulies

Music by Joseph J. Lilley

Vocal accompaniment by
The Jordanaires

Choreographed by
David Winters

Released March 22, 1967

Top: *Dodie Marshall and Elvis prepare for a scene in a wacky dune buggie custom-decorated for the film.* Bottom: *Elvis performs a 1960s-style number in the Easy Go-Go nightclub.*

THE FILMS OF ELVIS PRESLEY

DOUBLE TROUBLE

Double Trouble *spoofed spy thrillers, which were popular during the 1960s. The Wiere Brothers played inept government agents who revealed more secrets than they uncovered.*

STORYLINE

Taking advantage of the latest craze for discotheque dancing and the popularity of spy movies during the mid-1960s, the producers of *Double Trouble* combined the two fads to form the basic plot of this mediocre Elvis musical. Elvis walks through the role of Guy Lambert, a pop singer who becomes involved with intrigue while playing the discotheque scene in London and Antwerp. Guy's problems begin when he meets heiress Jill Conway, played by young Annette Day, who has a crush on the singer —much to the chagrin of her guardian. Jill leads Guy through numerous adventures involving spies, counterspies, jewel thieves, and harebrained detectives. The latter, played by the zany Wiere Brothers, provide the film's comic relief. Eventually, Jill succeeds in casting her spell over Guy, and the two marry.

BEHIND THE SCENES

One of the youngest actresses to ever costar with Elvis, English ingenue Annette Day was just 18 years old when she acted in *Double Trouble*. Day was discovered in typical Hollywood fashion. Producer Judd Bernard was shopping in an antique store on London's famed Portobello Road when he caught a glimpse of the red-haired teenager. The shop belonged to Day's mother, and Day was working behind the counter that day. Months later, when Bernard was casting for the film, he remembered the perky girl and called on her to ask the fateful question, "Do you want to be an actress?" After a script reading in London and some meetings with MGM executives, Day did a screen test in Hollywood, which satisfied the producers enough to cast her opposite Elvis. Her only prior acting experience had consisted of doing the Charleston in a Christmas concert at school. Elvis did take an interest in Day during filming, though not in the romantic sense. He surprised her near the end of shooting with a white Mustang as a remembrance of her first film experience.

CAST

Guy Lambert . . . .Elvis Presley
Jill Conway. . . . .Annette Day
Gerald Waverly . John Williams
Claire Dunham . . . .
. . . . .Yvonne Romain
Harry, a Belgian Detective . . .
. . . . .Harry Wiere
Herbert, a Belgian Detective . .
. . . . .Herbert Wiere
Sylvester, a Belgian Detective . .
. . . . .Sylvester Wiere
Archie Brown. . .Chips Rafferty
Arthur Babcock. . . . . . .
. . . . .Norman Rossington
Georgie . . . .Monty Landis
Morley . . . .Michael Murphy
Inspector De Groote . . . . .
. . . . .Leon Askin
Iceman . . . .John Alderson
Captain Roach . .Stanley Adams
Frenchman . . .Maurice Marsac
Mate. . . . . .Walter Burke
Twins at London Nightclub . . .
. .Marilyn and Melody Keymer
Bit. . . . . . .George Klein

CREDITS

Metro-Goldwyn-Mayer

Produced by Judd Bernard and
Irwin Winkler

Directed by Norman Taurog

Screenplay by Jo Heims

Based on a story by
Marc Brandel

Photographed in Metrocolor
and Panavision by
Daniel L. Fapp

Music by Jeff Alexander

Released April 5, 1967

Top: Double Trouble *was set in England and Belgium, but all scenes were shot at the MGM studio.*
Bottom: *Elvis's costar, young Annette Day, was still a teenager at the time of production.*

THE FILMS OF ELVIS PRESLEY

CLAMBAKE

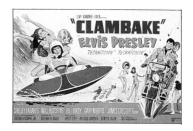

Clambake was originally titled Too Big for Texas.

SONGS

Clambake

Who Needs Money

A House That Has Everything

Confidence

You Don't Know Me

Hey, Hey, Hey

The Girl I Never Loved

Elvis serenades Shelley Fabares with "The Girl I Never Loved."

STORYLINE

In this "Prince and the Pauper" tale with a contemporary twist, Elvis portrays Scott Heyward, the son of a Texas oil baron. While in Miami, Scott meets penniless Tom Wilson, played by Will Hutchins, at a local snack bar. Determined to make it without using his wealthy father's name, Scott persuades Tom to switch identities with him. Scott takes over as the new water-ski instructor at a swank hotel, while Tom lives it up masquerading as the son of a millionaire. Bill Bixby costars as James J. Jamison III, a wealthy playboy who has won the Orange Bowl International Power Boat Regatta for three straight years. Scott sets out to defeat Jamison in the upcoming Regatta by teaming up with a local speedboat designer. The rivalry between Scott and Jamison is heightened by their mutual interest in beautiful Dianne Carter, played by Shelley Fabares, who claims to prefer Jamison because of his money. Scott reveals his true identity only after he wins the Regatta and the affections of Dianne.

BEHIND THE SCENES

Clambake was plagued by misfortune and chaos even before shooting started, and much of it was due to Elvis's total disinterest in doing the film. Depressed at being forced to make another zany musical comedy, Elvis experienced a major weight gain. United Artists demanded he take off the extra poundage. On the first day of scheduled shooting, Elvis slipped on his bathroom floor and hit his head. After a private conference with the Colonel, the doctor declared that Elvis had suffered a concussion and could not work. Shooting was delayed for more than two weeks. Bored with his films, Elvis and the Memphis Mafia resorted to crazier and crazier antics with each production. By the time *Clambake* rolled around, the group seemed out of control. Pie-throwings, firecracker fights, and water bombardments on the set were a common occurrence. MGM sent down a memo just before the shooting of the next Presley film, *Stay Away, Joe*, warning the group about their behavior.

CAST

Scott Heyward . . . .Elvis Presley
Dianne Carter . .Shelley Fabares
Tom Wilson . . .Will Hutchins
James J. Jamison III . .Bill Bixby
Duster Heyward. . . . . . .
. . . . . . .James Gregory
Sam Burton . . . .Gary Merrill
Ellie . . . . . .Amanda Harley
Sally . . . . . . .Suzie Kaye
Gloria . . .Angelique Pettyjohn
Gigi . . . . .Olga Kaya
Olive . . . . . .Arlene Charles
Mr. Hathaway . . . .Jack Good
Hal, the Doorman . .Hal Peary
Race Announcer. . .Sam Riddle
Lisa . . . . . . .Lisa Slagle
Bartender . . . . .Lee Krieger
Ice Cream Vendor . . .Red West
Mr. Heyward's Barber . . . . .
. . . . .Charlie Hodge
Bit . . . . . . .Joe Esposito
Bit. .Francis Humphrey Howard

CREDITS

United Artists

Produced by
Arnold Laven, Arthur Gardner,
and Jules Levy

Directed by Arthur H. Nadel

Screenplay by
Arthur Browne, Jr.

Photographed in Technicolor
and Techniscope by
William Margulies

Music by Jeff Alexander

Vocal accompaniment by
The Jordanaires

Released November 22, 1967

Top: *Will Hutchins changes places with millionaire Elvis.* Bottom: *Elvis performs "Confidence."*
Elvis's friend and bodyguard Red West was cast as the ice-cream vendor (right).

THE FILMS OF ELVIS PRESLEY

STAY AWAY, JOE

Elvis relaxes behind the scenes with manager Tom Parker (left) and wife Priscilla (right).

SONGS

Stay Away

Stay Away, Joe

Dominick

All I Needed Was the Rain

A fan snapped this rare candid of Elvis as he bought a Coke and a magazine at a liquor store near the film's location.

STORYLINE

Elvis played a Native American for the second time in his career in this musical comedy based on a best-selling book by Dan Cushman. This time, however, instead of being a relevant commentary on prejudice—as was the superior *Flaming Star*—the film stereotypes American Indians as shiftless and irresponsible. Elvis stars as rodeo rider Joe Lightcloud, a Navajo whose family still lives on the reservation. Joe persuades his congressman to give him 20 heifers and a prize bull so he and his father, played by Burgess Meredith, can prove that the Navajos can successfully raise cattle on the reservation. If their experiment is successful, then the government will help all the Navajo people. But Joe's buddy accidentally barbecues the prize bull, while Joe sells the heifers to buy plumbing and other home improvements for his stepmother, portrayed by Katy Jurado. Former leading lady Joan Blondell appears as tavern owner Glenda Callahan, whose daughter, played by Quentin Dean, can't seem to stay away from the girl-chasing Joe.

BEHIND THE SCENES

Stay Away, Joe provides another example of a Presley vehicle bolstered by a supporting cast of talented veterans. One of these veterans was Katy Jurado, who had built her career around playing sensuous exotic leads or juicy supporting roles. Her role as Elvis's stepmother in *Stay Away, Joe* represented her first major appearance in a comedy. Jurado brought a great deal more to the character of Annie Lightcloud than the producers had requested. The dedicated actress gained over 20 pounds to make her appearance more believable. Just prior to shooting, Jurado broke some bones in her foot. Unbeknown to the producer or director, she removed the cast before clearing it with her doctor. Consequently, her character walked with a limp. When asked, Jurado declared that the limp was part of her characterization. No one questioned her about it!

CAST

Joe Lightcloud . . .Elvis Presley
Charlie Lightcloud. . . . . . .
. . . . . . .Burgess Meredith
Glenda Callahan . .Joan Blondell
Annie Lightcloud . .Katy Jurado
Grandpa (Chief Lightcloud) . . .
. . . . .Thomas Gomez
Hy Slager . . . . .Henry Jones
Bronc Hoverty . . . .L.Q. Jones
Mamie Callahan. . . . . . .
. . . . .Quentin Dean
Mrs. Hawkins . .Anne Seymour
Congressman Morrissey . . . .
. . . . .Douglas Henderson
Lorne Hawkins. .Angus Duncan
Frank Hawk . . .Michael Lane
Mary Lightcloud. . . . . . .
. . . . .Susan Trustman
Hike Bowers . .Warren Vanders
Bull Shortgun . .Buck Kartalian
Connie Shortgun . . .Maurishka
Marlene Standing Rattle . . . .
. . . . .Caitlin Wyles
Billie Jo Hump . . . .
. . . . .Marya Christen
Car Salesman . . .Dick Wilson
Workman . . . . .Joe Esposito

CREDITS

Metro-Goldwyn-Mayer

Produced by Douglas Lawrence

Directed by Peter Tewksbury

Screenplay by Michael A. Hoey

Based on the novel by
Dan Cushman

Photographed in Metrocolor
and Panavision by
Fred Koenekamp

Music by Jack Marshall

Vocal accompaniment by
The Jordanaires

Released March 8, 1968

Top: *Elvis starred as Native American Joe Lightcloud in* Stay Away, Joe. *Bottom: Elvis and Quentin Dean clinch for the camera as veteran actress Joan Blondell looks on.*

THE FILMS OF ELVIS PRESLEY

SPEEDWAY

This soundtrack was the last RCA Presley album to be distributed in both mono and stereo.

SONGS

Speedway

Let Yourself Go

Your Time Hasn't Come Yet, Baby

He's Your Uncle, Not Your Dad

Who Are You? (Who Am I?)

There Ain't Nothing Like a Song

Your Groovy Self
(sung by Sinatra's character)

Elvis busses pal Nancy Sinatra while Bill Bixby looks on.

STORYLINE

Elvis's pals Nancy Sinatra and Bill Bixby costar in this musical comedy that features Elvis as stock-car champion Steve Grayson, a generous soul who is always sharing his winnings with people in need. Partly due to his generosity and partly because of his manager's love of gambling, Steve finds himself owing the government back taxes. Sinatra costars as IRS agent Susan Jacks, while Bixby plays his bumbling manager, Kenny Donford. Susan attempts to put Steve on a budget that will allow him to pay off the government in installments. Steve tries to soften the all-business agent with romance and music, but she thinks him frivolous and irresponsible. But her tune changes when she realizes that Steve's latest charity case is a former stock-car driver with five daughters who has fallen on hard times. Eventually Susan is able to keep Steve on a budget, while Steve is able to keep Susan on his arm.

BEHIND THE SCENES

Nancy Sinatra's friendship with Elvis dated back to 1960 when she met him at the airport upon his return from Germany to be discharged from the Army. Nancy presented him with some shirts as a gift from her famous father. Though the gesture fueled rumors of a romance between the two, chances are it was meant to promote Frank Sinatra's upcoming TV special featuring Elvis, Frank Sinatra's Rat Pack, and Nancy. Elvis and Nancy did not work together again until 1967 when they began shooting *Speedway*. Elvis had married Priscilla Beaulieu a few weeks earlier, but rumors began to fly that he and Nancy were having a relationship. Fanzines had a field day with the rumors. "Will Nancy Sinatra Steal Elvis from Priscilla?" and "How Can Elvis Resist his Sexy Costar?" blared the headlines. Testament to their friendship is indicated by the inclusion of Nancy's song, "Your Groovy Self" on the *Speedway* soundtrack, marking the only time a solo by another singer appeared on a regular Presley album.

CAST

Steve Grayson . . . .Elvis Presley
Susan Jacks. . . .Nancy Sinatra
Kenny Donford . . . .Bill Bixby
R.W. Hepworth . .Gale Gordon
Abel Esterlake . . . .
. . . . . .William Schallert
Ellie Esterlake. . . . .
. . . . . . .Victoria Meyerink
Paul Dado . . . . .Ross Hagen
Birdie Kebner . .Carl Ballantine
Juan Medala. . . .Poncie Ponce
The Cook . . . .Harry Hickox
Miss Charlotte Speedway . .Miss
Beverly Hills (Mary Ann Ashman)
Debbie Esterlake . . . .
. . . . . .Michele Newman
Carrie Esterlake. . . . .
. . . . .Courtney Brown
Billie Esterlake . . .Dana Brown
Annie Esterlake . . . .
. . . . .Patti Jean Keith
Janitor at the Coffee Shop. . . .
. . . . .Burt Mustin
Guitarist. . . . .Charlie Hodge
Stock-Car Racers . . . .Richard
Petty, Buddy Baker, Cale Yarbo-
rough, Dick Hutcherson, Tiny
Lund, G.C. Spencer, Roy Mayne

CREDITS

Metro-Goldwyn-Mayer
Produced by Douglas Laurence
Directed by Norman Taurog
Screenplay by Phillip Shuken
Photographed in Metrocolor
and Panavision by
Joseph Ruttenberg
Music by Jeff Alexander
Vocal accompaniment by
The Jordanaires
Released June 12, 1968

Top: *Costar Nancy Sinatra and Elvis were good friends in real life.* Bottom: *Elvis and Nancy Sinatra join in a duet for* Speedway's *raucous final number, "There Ain't Nothing Like a Song."*

THE FILMS OF ELVIS PRESLEY

LIVE A LITTLE,
LOVE A LITTLE

While filming, Rudy Vallee (left) was mobbed by senior citizens who knocked down Elvis to get Vallee's autograph.

SONGS

Wonderful World

Edge of Reality

A Little Less Conversation

Almost in Love

Michele Carey's role was an attempt to update Elvis's musicals.

STORYLINE

In an attempt to keep up with the changing times, the producers of this comedy created a slightly different Elvis Presley film. *Live a Little, Love a Little* featured a franker approach to sex than previous Elvis comedies. It also made use of kookier characters who were devoid of the sentimentality of his earlier films, and it included a psychedelic-type production number called "Edge of Reality." Elvis stars as photographer Greg Nolan, who earns his living by working for two very distinct clients. Mike Landsdown, played by Don Porter, owns and operates Classic Cat Magazine, a girlie publication that features titillating photos. Louis Penlow, played by Rudy Vallee, owns a tasteful advertising agency that prides itself on its classy photography. Neither client knows Greg is working for the other. When Greg is not hopping back and forth between photo assignments, he is trying to get freewheeling and free-loving Bernice, played by Michele Carey, out of his hair.

BEHIND THE SCENES

Elvis's management team, as well as the producers at MGM, were aware that the singer's image had not kept pace with the fast-changing 1960s. Producer Hal Wallis had chosen not to renew Elvis's contract when it expired in 1967 because, as Wallis noted, "It's not so much that Elvis is changing, but that the times are changing. There's just not the market for the no-plot musicals that there once was." Billed as a comedy rather than a musical comedy, *Live a Little* was fashioned after the hip sex farces of the 1960s, such as *The Swinger* and *A Guide for the Married Man*. Though not as wild as some films from the era, it did feature Elvis's character swearing. Also, the script makes clear that the character of Bernice had been sexually active prior to meeting Greg; near the end of the film, Greg and Bernice sleep together without benefit of marriage. Though the story ends with a marriage proposal, the franker attitude toward sex was a surprise to some critics and audience members.

CAST

Greg Nolan . . . . .Elvis Presley
Bernice . . . . .Michele Carey
Mike Landsdown . .Don Porter
Louis Penlow . . . .Rudy Vallee
Harry. . . . . .Dick Sargent
Milkman . . .Sterling Holloway
Ellen . . . . . .Celeste Yarnall
Delivery Boy . . .Eddie Hodges
Robbie's Mother . .Joan Shawlee
Miss Selfridge . . .Mary Grover
Receptionist . . . .Emily Banks
Art Director . . .Michael Keller
1st Secretary . . . .Merri Ashley
2nd Secretary . . .Phyllis Davis
Perfume Model . .Ursula Menzel
Robbie . . . . .John Hegner
Sally, the Mermaid Model. . . .
. . . . . . .Susan Henning
Newspaper Employees . . . . .
. . . . .Red West, Sonny West

CREDITS

Metro-Goldwyn-Mayer

Produced by Douglas Laurence

Directed by Norman Taurog

Screenplay by Michael A. Hoey
and Dan Greenburg

Photographed in Metrocolor
and Panavision by
Fred Koenekamp

Music by Billy Strange

Choreography by
Jack Regas and Jack Baker

Released October 23, 1968

Top: *Although Michele Carey and Elvis share a bed, it's all kept innocent with a bed divider.*
Bottom: *Dick Sargent (left) and Elvis vie for the affections of Michele Carey.*

THE FILMS OF ELVIS PRESLEY

Jess Wade . . . . . .Elvis Presley
Tracy Winters . . . . .Ina Balin
Vince Hackett . . .Victor French
Marcie . . . . . .Lynn Kellogg
Sara Ramsey . . .Barbara Werle
Billy Roy Hackett . . . . . .
. . . . .Solomon Sturges
Opie Keetch . . .Paul Brinegar
Gunner . . . . .James Sikking
Heff . . . . . .Harry Landers
Lieutenant Rivera . .Tony Young
Sheriff Dan Ramsey . . . . . .
. . . . .James Almanzar
Mody . . . . .Charles H. Gray
Lige. . . . . . .Rodd Redwing
Martin Tilford . .Garry Walberg
Gabe . . . . . . .Duane Grey
Henry Carter . . . .
. . . . . .J. Edward McKinley
Jerome Selby. . . .John Pickard
Will Joslyn . . . .Robert Luster
Christa . . . . . .Christa Lang
Mexican Peon . .Charlie Hodge

National General Pictures

Produced by Harry Caplan
and Charles Marquis Warren

Directed by
Charles Marquis Warren

Screenplay by
Charles Marquis Warren

Based on a story by
Frederic Louis Fox

Photographed in Technicolor
and Panavision by
Ellsworth Fredericks

Music by Hugo Montenegro

Released March 13, 1969

Elvis played a western antihero who was costumed similarly to the character Clint Eastwood portrayed in several Italian westerns.

CHARRO!

Sporting a beard and a tough demeanor, Elvis stars as Jess Wade in this offbeat western that features no musical numbers. The minimal storyline finds Wade, a reformed badman, pitted against the members of his old gang. The gang is now led by Vince Hackett, played by character actor Victor French, who takes delight in terrorizing a small Mexican town. The gang has stolen from the town a gold-plated cannon that was used by Emperor Maximilian in his ill-fated fight against popular Mexican leader Benito Juarez. The gang's motive is to force a ransom from the town for the cannon, but the gang also uses the cannon to hold the townspeople at bay. Only Wade can save the people from his former gang. European star Ina Balin costars as Tracy Winters, a dance hall hostess in love with Wade.

BEHIND THE SCENES

With its gritty look, violent antihero, and cynical point of view, *Charro!* was obviously patterned after the grim Italian westerns of the 1960s. Elvis's character, Jess Wade, is costumed similarly to Clint Eastwood's notorious "Man with No Name" from Sergio Leone's Italian westerns. Both wore a scruffy beard and dust-covered western garb, and both kept a well-worn cigar in their mouths. The music in *Charro!* was scored by Hugo Montenegro, who was responsible for the memorable score of *The Good, the Bad, and the Ugly.* Unfortunately, director Charles Marquis Warren was no match for Sergio Leone, and *Charro!* suffers from poor production values.

At the time, much was made about the absence of songs in the film, as though that fact proved *Charro!* was a serious effort. Advertisements for the film declared *Charro!* featured "a different kind of role . . . a different kind of man." Elvis granted more interviews and generated more publicity for *Charro!* than he had for any film in a long time. One interview quoted him as saying, "*Charro!* is the first movie I ever made

Advertising emphasized that Charro! *represented a radical departure for Elvis.*

SONGS

Charro

Throughout his career, Elvis was always willing to accommodate fans with autographs and photos.

without singing a song. I play a gunfighter, and I just couldn't see a singing gunfighter." Eventually, Elvis did agree to sing the title tune, but there are no songs within the body of the film.

Charro! was filmed in the late summer of 1968 after Elvis's comeback special had been shot for television, though the special would not air until December. Elvis seemed to have taken stock of his career that year: He recorded music that was not merely fodder for soundtrack albums, and he starred in a prestigious television special. Perhaps Elvis was hoping to upgrade his acting career as well by appearing in a completely different type of film. Unfortunately, the film was a dismal critical failure; much of the blame was placed at the feet of director Charles Marquis Warren.

Warren had been a writer, director, and producer for several western television series during the 1960s. Though he had not worked in the cinema since the 1950s, he chose to produce, direct, and write the screenplay for *Charro!*

Elvis seems to have gotten along well with Warren despite an incident that occurred on the set. One morning, Elvis was practicing his quick draw for an upcoming scene. Not realizing one of the guns was loaded with blanks, Elvis accidentally fired a gun into Warren's face at a range of one yard. Luckily, the gun had only a quarter-load blank charge, and the director received only minor powder burns and cracked glasses. After receiving first aid on the set, Warren returned to direct that day. According to witnesses, Elvis was much more upset than Warren about the accident, so Warren began joking with him. "Well, at least now I know what you think of your director," he kidded.

Fewer shenanigans involving Elvis and his buddy-bodyguards were reported from the set of *Charro!* than was typical for a Presley film. Many of the film's crew and some members of the Memphis Mafia grew beards to match Elvis's while the film was in production. Even Colonel Parker grew a beard, but he chose to shave his when he returned home to his wife, Marie.

A number of television actors costarred in Charro! *James Sikking (holding Elvis's arms) is best known for his role on the series* Hill Street Blues.

Charro! *featured only one song, the title tune, which was sung over the opening credits.*

Ina Balin costarred with Elvis in one of her few film roles.

Top: *The original title for* Charro! *was* Come Hell, Come Sundown. Bottom: *The film was shot on location in and around Arizona's Superstition Mountains.*

THE TROUBLE WITH GIRLS

About 450 extras were used in the parade scenes, including 100 children.

SONGS

Swing Low, Sweet Chariot

The Whiffenpoof Song

Violet (Flower of NYU)

Clean Up Your Own Backyard

Sign of the Zodiac

Almost

A dapper Elvis looks happy in this publicity still, perhaps realizing that his movie contracts were about to expire.

STORYLINE

An odd mixture of music, comedy, and melodrama, *The Trouble with Girls* is unique for a Presley picture because Elvis is only on screen for about a third of the film. Elvis stars as Walter Hale, the manager of a traveling chautauqua. A chautauqua is a school that provides education combined with entertainment. Walter is beset with a number of problems as his show arrives in town for one week. He worries that he might have to give the mayor's untalented daughter the lead in the children's pageant to stay in the mayor's good graces. He must contend with his assistant, played by Marlyn Mason, who is constantly harping about the union rights of his employees. Finally, someone murders the local druggist, and a member of the chautauqua is accused. These loose ends are tied together during the final show, when Walter cannily reveals the killer's identity and wins the heart of his pretty assistant.

BEHIND THE SCENES

The Trouble with Girls had a long history of trying to reach the screen. In June 1959, trade magazines announced that Don Mankiewicz was set to write a sceenplay based on an unpublished story by Mauri Grashin, Day Keene, and Dwight Babcock. The film was tentatively titled *Chautauqua*. In December 1960, MGM announced that Glenn Ford was slated to star in *Chautauqua* with Elvis Presley, Hope Lange, and Arthur O'Connell. Valentine Davies was scheduled to adapt the story. The following year, only Elvis remained in the original cast, and William Wister Haines was doing the adaptation of the story, which Keene and Babcock had recently published as a novel. By 1964, Dick Van Dyke was announced as the star of *Chautauqua*. Many writers later, the property was sold to Columbia Pictures. Van Dyke was still scheduled to be the star, but the title had been changed to *Big America*. In April 1968, the property was resold to MGM, where it was adapted as an Elvis Presley vehicle by Arnold and Lois Peyser.

CAST

Walter Hale . . . . .Elvis Presley
Charlene. . . . .Marlyn Mason
Betty . . . . . . .Nicole Jaffe
Nita Bix . . . .Sheree North
Johnny . . . .Edward Andrews
Mr. Drewcolt . .John Carradine
Mr. Jonson (Mr. Morality). . . .
. . . . .Vincent Price
Carol Bix . . . . .Anissa Jones
Maude. . . . .Joyce Van Patten
Willy . . . . . . .Pepe Brown
Harrison Wilby . . . .
. . . . . .Dabney Coleman
Mayor Gilchrist. . .Bill Zuckert
Mr. Perper . . . . .Pitt Herbert
Boy with Yale Sweater . . . . .
. . . . .Kevin O'Neal
Boy with Princeton Sweater . . .
. . . . .John Rubenstein
Boy with Rutgers Sweater . . . .
. . . . .Frank Welker
Boy with Amherst Sweater . . .
. . . . .Chuck Briles
Deputy Sheriff . .Jerry Schilling
Gambler . . . . .Joe Esposito
Vocal Group . .The Jordanaires

CREDITS

Metro-Goldwyn-Mayer

Produced by Lester Welch

Directed by Peter Tewksbury

Screenplay by
Arnold and Lois Peyser

Based on a story by
Mauri Grashin, Day Keene, and
Dwight Babcock

Based on a novel by
Day Keene and Dwight Babcock

Photographed in Metrocolor
and Panavision by
Jacques Marquette

Music by Billy Strange

Released September 3, 1969

Top: *Marlyn Mason made her film debut in* The Trouble with Girls. *Bottom: (from left) Anissa Jones, Pepe Brown, Marlyn Mason, and Elvis perform for the Chautauqua.*

THE FILMS OF ELVIS PRESLEY

CHANGE OF HABIT

This soundtrack album was not released with the film; quite possibly, it is a bootleg album.

SONGS

Change of Habit

Rubberneckin'

Have a Happy

Let Us Pray

Elvis's three costars were (from left) Jane Elliot, Mary Tyler Moore, and singer Barbara McNair.

STORYLINE

Ending his days in Hollywood with the type of dramatic role Elvis always craved gives an ironic twist to his movie career. Though not a particularly profound film, *Change of Habit* does represent a change of venue for Elvis. A drama instead of a comedy, the film featured only three songs. As Dr. John Carpenter, Elvis stars as a professional man for the first time in his career. Dr. Carpenter heads a clinic in a ghetto area of a major metropolis. He is surprised to be offered assistance by three women. Unknown to him, the three are nuns in street clothing who want to aid the community but are afraid the local residents might be reluctant to seek help if their true identities were known. Dr. Carpenter falls in love with Sister Michelle Gallagher, played by wholesome Mary Tyler Moore, but Sister Michelle's true vocation remains unknown to Dr. Carpenter. Sister Michelle also has feelings for the doctor, but she is reluctant to leave the order. The film concludes with Sister Michelle entering a church to pray for guidance to make her choice—the church or Dr. Carpenter.

BEHIND THE SCENES

Change of Habit was very loosely based on the story of Sister Mary Olivia Gibson, who worked with children afflicted with speech handicaps. Sister Mary Olivia headed the speech clinic at Maria Regina College in Syracuse, New York. Part of her therapy involved using variations on theatrical techniques. How much of her story was retained in the script was pondered by many critics in their reviews, but they all agreed that the material provided Elvis with a welcome change of pace. That it was too little too late was apparent by Elvis's lack of interest in pursuing a film career. He had let his film contracts expire, and *Change of Habit* was his last commitment. He was eagerly awaiting his freedom so that he could return to live performances.

CAST

Dr. John Carpenter . . . . . .
. . . . .Elvis Presley
Sister Michelle Gallagher . . . .
. . . . . .Mary Tyler Moore
Sister Irene Hawkins . . . . . .
. . . . .Barbara McNair
Sister Barbara Bennett . . . . .
. . . . .Jane Elliot
Mother Joseph . . .Leora Dana
Lieutenant Moretti. . . . . . .
. . . . .Edward Asner
The Banker . . .Robert Emhardt
Father Gibbons . .Regis Toomey
Rose . . . . . .Doro Merande
Lily. . . . . .Ruth McDevitt
Bishop Finley . . . .
. . . . . . .Richard Carlson
Julio Hernandez. . .Nefti Millet
Desiree . . . . .Laura Figueroa
Amanda Parker. . .Lorena Kirk
Miss Parker . .Virginia Vincent
Colom . . . . . .David Renard
Hawk. . . . . .Ji-Tu Cumbuka
Robbie . . . . . . .Bill Elliott
1st Young Man . . .Mario Aniov
2nd Young Man . . .A Martinez

CREDITS

Universal Pictures

Produced by Joe Connelly

Directed by William Graham

Screenplay by
James Lee, S.S. Schweitzer,
and Eric Bercovici

Based on a story by
John Joseph and Richard Morris

Photographed in Technicolor by
Russell Metty

Music by William Goldenberg

Released November 10, 1969

Top: *Mary Tyler Moore portrayed a nun in Elvis's last feature film.* Bottom: *In a departure from his usual role, Elvis played a doctor who practices in a free clinic for ghetto residents.*

THE FILMS OF ELVIS PRESLEY

ELVIS—THAT'S THE WAY IT IS

*Elvis's first concert film was
Elvis—That's the Way It Is.*

CREDITS

Metro-Goldwyn-Mayer

Produced by Herbert F. Soklow

Directed by Denis Sanders

Photographed by Lucien Ballard

Edited by Henry Berman

Elvis's wardrobe by Bill Belew

Musicians with Elvis:
James Burton,
Glen Hardin, Charlie Hodge,
Jerry Scheff, Ronnie Tutt, and
John Wilkinson

Orchestra conducted by
Joe Guercio

SEQUENCE OF EVENTS

Rather than a narrative feature, Elvis's 32nd film is a documentary chronicling his 1970 summer appearance at the International Hotel in Las Vegas. Elvis began rehearsals July 5 at the MGM studios in Hollywood, where he worked on his material for about a month. The show opened August 10. The MGM cameras not only recorded the rehearsals but also opening night, several performances throughout the engagement, and one show at Veterans Memorial Coliseum in Phoenix, Arizona. The film is structured so that the rehearsals and other scenes of preparation build to an extended climax of Elvis onstage. Dressed in a simple, white jumpsuit, accented with fringe instead of rhinestones and gems, Elvis is showcased at the pinnacle of his career.

BEHIND THE SCENES

According to the personal accounts of a couple of Elvis's buddy-bodyguards, Elvis received a death threat during this engagement at the International in the summer of 1970. A security guard at the hotel was notified on August 26 that Elvis would be kidnapped sometime that night. Feeling protected by extra security, Elvis chose to perform that night as usual. The next day, Colonel Parker's office received a similar warning over the phone. Again, Elvis performed that night as usual. On August 28, the wife of Joe Esposito, who was Elvis's foreman, received another threatening phone call at her home in Los Angeles. She was told that Elvis would be shot in the middle of that night's show. With armed bodyguards in the wings, and, according to some, a couple of guns tucked into his costume, Elvis honored that old show business tradition that declares the show must go on. The person or persons responsible for the odious threats were never apprehended.

Top: *Elvis stars in documentarist Denis Sanders's Oscar-winning film* Elvis—That's the Way It Is.
Bottom: *The camera captured Elvis in rehearsal for his August 1970 stint in Las Vegas.*

THE FILMS OF ELVIS PRESLEY

ELVIS ON TOUR

Long before he became one of America's best directors, a young Martin Scorsese supervised part of the editing for Elvis on Tour.

CREDITS

Metro-Goldwyn-Mayer

Produced and directed by
Pierre Adidge and Robert Abel

Photographed by Robert Thomas

Musicians with Elvis:
James Burton,
Charlie Hodge, Ronnie Tutt,
Glen Hardin, Jerry Scheff, and
John Wilkinson

Orchestra conducted by
Joe Guercio

Background vocals by
Kathy Westmoreland,
The Sweet Inspirations, and
J.D. Sumner
and the Stamps Quartet

SEQUENCE OF EVENTS

The second documentary to capture Elvis in performance focused on his road show. *Elvis on Tour* chronicled the singer's extensive 15-city tour in the spring of 1972. The tour started in Buffalo, New York, and came to a rousing conclusion in Albuquerque, New Mexico. Much of the tour centered in the South. In addition to the concert footage of Elvis, the film attempted to reveal the real Elvis Presley backstage and off-guard. A camera followed the singer and his entourage, while Elvis was asked to comment on such topics as his music and his childhood. *Elvis on Tour* did not present the real Elvis, it only added to the myth that surrounded him. Despite the filmmakers' intentions, Elvis would drop no veils. In lieu of a revealing portrait, the filmmakers succeeded in capturing the hectic pace of Elvis's tour through a montage sequence of cities visited during the tour. A collection of clips from his movies in which Elvis kisses a number of his costars adds a touch of humor.

BEHIND THE SCENES

Costing $600,000 to produce (not including Elvis's fee of $1 million), *Elvis on Tour* recouped its production costs after three days in the theaters. Documentaries are rarely major box-office draws, but this film was a financial success. Critically acclaimed as well, *Elvis on Tour* won a Golden Globe as the Best Documentary of 1972. Elvis himself kept track of the awards ceremony the evening the Golden Globes were passed out, and he shouted with pride when the film won. Much of the creative success of the film was due to its effective editing style, which relied on a split-screen technique to convey the excitement of Elvis in concert. Multiple images of Elvis performing were shown simultaneously on the screen. The series of scenes from Elvis's movies plus the succession of clips of the different cities visited on the tour also depended on precise editing for its visual impact. In charge of these montage sequences was a young filmmaker named Martin Scorsese.

(credits continued)

Opening act by Jackie Kahane

Edited by Ken Zemke

Montage supervised by
Martin Scorsese

Research by Andrew Solt,
Carole Kismaric, and
Jack Goelman

Elvis's wardrobe by Bill Belew

SONGS INCLUDED

Johnny B. Goode

See See Rider

Polk Salad Annie

Separate Ways

Proud Mary

Never Been to Spain

Burning Love

That's All Right (Mama)

Lead Me, Guide Me

Bosom of Abraham

Love Me Tender

Until It's Time for You to Go

Suspicious Minds

I, John

Bridge Over Troubled Water

Funny How Time Slips Away

An American Trilogy

Mystery Train

I Got a Woman/Amen

A Big Hunk o' Love

You Gave Me a Mountain

Lawdy Miss Clawdy

Can't Help Falling in Love

Memories

Lighthouse
(sung by J.D. Sumner and
the Stamps Quartet)

Sweet Sweet Spirit
(sung by J.D. Sumner and
the Stamps Quartet)

Top: *This second concert documentary of Elvis focused on a 15-city tour in April 1972.*
Bottom: *Elvis clowns for the camera by turning his sunglasses upside down.*

THE FILMS OF ELVIS PRESLEY

Elvis on the set of Loving You.